Basic Grammar *in use*

WORKBOOK

with answers

William R. Smalzer

with Raymond Murphy

CAMBRIDGE UNIVERSITY PRESS
Cambridge, New York, Melbourne, Madrid, Cape Town, Singapore, São Paulo, Delhi

Cambridge University Press
32 Avenue of the Americas, New York, NY 10013–2473, USA

www.cambridge.org
Information on this title: www.cambridge.org/9780521797184

First published 2003
13th printing 2008

Printed in Hong Kong, China, by Golden Cup Printing Company Limited

A catalog record for this publication is available from the British Library

ISBN 978-0-521-62600-2 pack consisting of student's book with answers and audio CD
ISBN 978-0-521-62599-9 pack consisting of student's book without answers and audio CD
ISBN 978-0-521-52877-1 student's book with answers/Korea
ISBN 978-0-521-79718-4 workbook with answers
ISBN 978-0-521-79717-7 workbook without answers

Art direction, book design, photo research and layout services: Adventure House, NYC
Illustrations: Randy Jones and Susann Ferris Jones

Contents

To the Student

Basic Grammar in Use Workbook provides you with practice in North American English, building on grammar points presented and practiced in the *Basic Grammar in Use* student's book. It offers additional exercises on difficult grammar points and a variety of exercises. The workbook will help you apply what you have learned in the student's book.

The workbook covers the same grammar points as the student's book. The types of exercises in the workbook are often different from those in the student's book, however. This way you can use what you have learned in a slightly different way. The exercises in this workbook will also help you understand how the grammar points in one unit of the student's book are related to the grammar in other units. You may be asked to use several different grammar structures in one exercise.

In general, workbook exercises will require you to read longer passages and write longer answers than the exercises in the student's book. In some exercises, you will rewrite whole sentences using different grammar structures but keeping the same meaning. In other exercises, you will read paragraphs and fill in blanks with correct forms. In review exercises, you will have the chance to write sentences using your own ideas.

Level

Like the student's book, the *Basic Grammar in Use Workbook* is intended for beginning and low-intermediate students. However, intermediate learners who have problems with grammar will also find the book useful.

How the workbook is organized

There are 137 exercises covering all 116 units in the student's book. One exercise in the workbook may cover the grammar in one, two, or three units in the student's book, however. Each exercise has a heading that tells which units of the student's book are covered in that exercise. Workbook exercises are grouped into sections, according to the sections in the student's book (see the Contents). At the end of most sections, there are review exercises.

How to use the workbook

Use the workbook after you have completed the corresponding units in the student's book. If you have trouble with the exercises on the right-hand pages of the student's book, review the explanations on the left-hand pages of those units. Then do the workbook exercises for those units.

Checking your work

After you have done an exercise or group of exercises in the workbook, check your answers in the Answer Key at the back of the book. You can use the Answer Key in several different ways:

Students working alone

Check your answers at the back of the book.

Students working in pairs

Student A: Read your answers to Student B, who will tell you if they are correct.

Student B: Check the key as you listen to Student A answer each item. In case of errors, try to help your partner find the correct solution rather than just reading it.

Groups of four or more (working in pairs)

Work with a partner on an exercise. Decide on your answers together. When you finish, compare answers with another pair of students. Discuss any differences. Finally, check the Answer Key together.

Groups of four or more (working with a leader)

Choose a leader. The leader opens the book to the Answer Key. The other group members take turns reading their answers. For each answer, group members compare their own answers to the one they heard, discussing any differences. The leader, after listening to other members, reads the correct answer.

If you do not understand an answer in the Answer Key, ask your teacher or someone who knows English well to explain the answer to you. Exercises that ask you to use your own ideas have sample answers. Your answers will of course be different. If you are studying in a class, your teacher may check your answers to those exercises.

To the Teacher

Basic Grammar in Use Workbook provides exercises to reinforce and extend the grammar lessons presented and practiced in the *Basic Grammar in Use* student's book. An exercise in the workbook often covers more than one unit in the student's book, in order to help students consolidate their knowledge of related grammar points. Thus, workbook exercises are often slightly more challenging than exercises in the student's book, in addition to having more varied formats.

The workbook covers all 116 units in the student's book. At the beginning of every workbook exercise is a heading that indicates the numbers and titles of the relevant units in the student's book. Intended to supplement the student's book, workbook exercises should be done after the relevant units in the student's book have been completed. Exercises in the workbook are organized into sections, corresponding to the sections in the Contents in the *Basic Grammar in Use* student's book. Review exercises can be found at the end of each section.

The book will be most useful for students at the beginning and low-intermediate levels. It will also be useful for intermediate students who need further practice on particular grammar points. Like the student's book, the workbook can be used by whole classes, by individual students needing extra help, or for independent study. Many of the exercises lend themselves better to writing than to oral work. These exercises may be done independently, or by students working together in the classroom.

The self-study edition of the workbook contains an answer key. Exercises that ask students to use their own ideas have sample answers. Students' actual answers will of course vary. You might want to look over student answers to such exercises at intervals, or have students share their answers in class. A classroom edition of the *Basic Grammar in Use Workbook* without an answer key is also available.

Basic Grammar in use

WORKBOOK

with answers

EXERCISE 1

Am/is/are

Write sentences about the people in the picture. Begin the sentences with *he*, *she*, *they*, or *it* + *is/are*. Then use the words in the box.

angry	~~cold~~	happy	hungry	interested in cars
thirsty	tired	very heavy	very tall	hot

1. (Andy) _He's cold._ _____

2. (Sally) She _____ .

3. (Hannah and Jessica) They _____ .

4. (Ted) _____

5. (Mike and Carlos) _____

6. (Josh) _____

7. (Christina) _____

8. (Katie and Sarah) _____

9. (Teacher) _____

10. (Brandon's bookbag) _____

EXERCISE 2

Am/is/are

Write two sentences to answer each question: a positive sentence and a negative sentence.

1. Which is a big country? (Latvia, Russia)

   Russia is a big country.

   Latvia isn't a big country.

2. Which ones are warm countries? (Saudi Arabia, Finland, Poland, Brazil)

   Saudi Arabia and Brazil are warm countries.

   Finland and _____ .

3. Which of these are expensive? (tea, diamonds, a newspaper)

   _____

   _____

4. Which of these cities are in Canada? (Atlanta, Vancouver, Toronto)

   _____

   _____

5. Are you married or single?

   _____

   _____

6. Which of these cities are in South America? (Madrid, Santiago, Lima, Buenos Aires)

   _____

   _____

7. Which are necessary for a cake? (eggs, butter, pepper, sugar)

   _____

   _____

8. Are you and your family from Brazil or from another country?

   We _____ .

   _____

EXERCISE 3

Am/is/are (Questions)

Write questions with the words in parentheses and *am*, *is*, or *are*. Use any other words that are necessary, and use question marks. Read the answers first.

Questions

1. (your parents) *Where are your parents?*
   _____

2. (you / cold) *Are you cold?*
   _____

3. (your friend / from Russia) _____
   _____

4. (your parents) _____
   _____

5. (Linda's apartment) _____
   _____

6. (tired) _____
   _____

7. (this postcard) _____
   _____

8. (Julia's hair) _____
   _____

9. (your teachers / nice) _____
   _____

10. (you) _____
    _____

11. (angry with me) _____
    _____

12. (those people) _____
    _____

13. (their names) _____
    _____

14. It looks cold outside. (right) _____
    _____

Answers

They're at home.

No, I'm fine.

No, she's from Poland.

They're fine, thanks.

It's on Third Street.

No, I'm not.

It's 25 cents.

It's red this week.

Yes, I think they are.

I'm 29.

Because you are always late!

They're my aunt and uncle.

Jeff and Alice Turner.

Yes, you're right. It is very cold.

I am doing (Present Continuous)

Look at each picture. Use the words in parentheses to write two sentences in the present continuous: a positive sentence and a negative sentence.

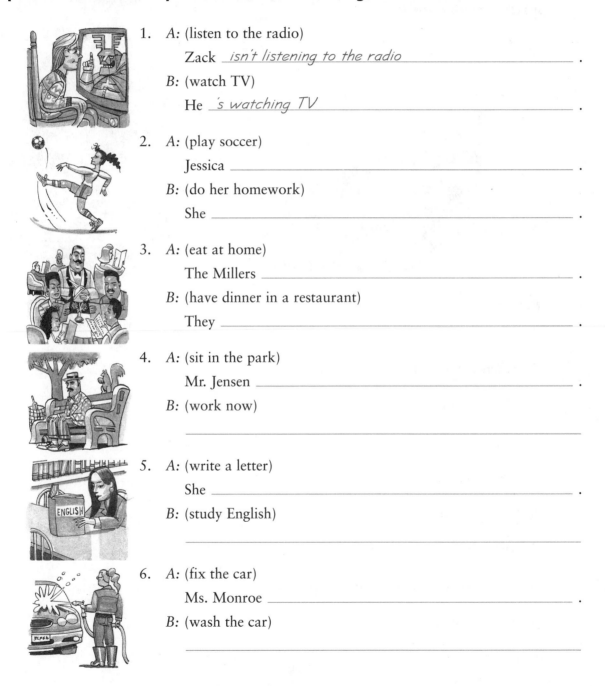

1. *A:* (listen to the radio)

   Zack *isn't listening to the radio* .

   B: (watch TV)

   He *'s watching TV* .

2. *A:* (play soccer)

   Jessica _____ .

   B: (do her homework)

   She _____ .

3. *A:* (eat at home)

   The Millers _____ .

   B: (have dinner in a restaurant)

   They _____ .

4. *A:* (sit in the park)

   Mr. Jensen _____ .

   B: (work now)

   _____ .

5. *A:* (write a letter)

   She _____ .

   B: (study English)

   _____ .

6. *A:* (fix the car)

   Ms. Monroe _____ .

   B: (wash the car)

   _____ .

Are you doing . . . ? (Present Continuous Questions)

A friend is visiting town and leaves a phone message. Write questions for your friend with the words in parentheses. (Note: Not all the questions will be in the present continuous.)

Hi. This is Sam Chung. It's about 10 in the morning, and we are in town for a day. We're leaving tomorrow. I want to see you. Are you busy?

Also, I need information on good places to visit in town. I'll call you again later today. Bye.

Questions for Sam

1. (why / leave / so soon) *Why are you leaving so soon?*

2. (where / stay) _____

3. (travel / with somebody) _____

4. (see / other friends here) _____

5. (how / enjoy / my town) _____

6. (how / get / around town) _____

7. (visit / famous places here) _____

8. (interested in art museums) _____

9. (where / now) _____

10. (what / do now) _____

I do, I work, I like, etc. (Simple Present)
I don't . . . (Negative Simple Present)

Use the words in parentheses, and write sentences that make sense with* the first sentence. Write positive or negative sentences as needed.

1. Mia isn't a good traveler.

   (like / different kinds of food) *She doesn't like different kinds of food.*

   (like / to sleep in her own bed) She *likes to sleep in her own bed* .

   (enjoy / new places) _____

   (know / other languages) _____

   (like / to take airplanes) _____

2. Andrew isn't in very good health*.

   (eat / healthy food) He _____ .

   (sleep / enough) _____

   (smoke / a lot) _____

3. Angela's and Paul's lives are hard.

   (make / a lot of money) They _____ .

   (live / in a very nice place) _____

   (have / boring jobs) _____

4. I have a lot of friends.

   (like to be with people) I _____ .

   (talk / about others behind their back*) _____

   (listen / to others' problems) _____

5. You are a very good boss.

   (listen / to your employees*) You _____ .

   (work / hard) _____

   (get / angry often) _____

* make sense with: *to go together logically*
* be in good health: *to be well*
* talk about others behind their back: *to say bad things about others when they are not there*
* employee: *someone who is paid to work for someone else*

Do you . . . ? (Simple Present Questions)

You meet a young woman from Quebec City, Canada. Write questions to ask her. Use the words in parentheses in the right order. Add necessary words. (Look at the answers first.)

Your questions	The woman's answers
1. (like / Quebec) *Do you like Quebec?*	Yes, I like it a lot.
2. (snow / it / a lot / there / in the winter) Does _____ ?	Yes, it does. And it's usually very cold.
3. (do / there) What _____ ?	I am a French teacher.
4. (teach / French as a second language) _____	No, I teach French as a first language.
5. (children in Quebec / study / French) _____	Yes. Most of them do.
6. (people in Quebec / speak / French) _____	Not everyone does, but most people do.
7. (students / have / in your class) How _____ ?	I have 20 in one class, and 25 in the other one.
8. (many tourists / visit / Quebec City) _____	Yes, a lot visit in the summer.
9. (teach / in the summer) _____	No, I'm usually free in the summer.
10. (take / a vacation every year) _____	Yes, I try to.
11. (go / usually) _____	I travel to other parts of Canada. Sometimes I go to the United States or South America.

UNIT
8

I am doing and *I do* (Present Continuous and Simple Present)

A. Answer the questions about the pictures. Write full sentences or short answers as needed.

1. Tanya	2. Sally	3. Isabel and Matt	4. You

Job: Russian teacher Hobby: playing the guitar	Job: mechanic Hobby: dancing	Job: computer programmers Hobby: playing chess	Job: ? Hobby: ?

1. a. Is Tanya teaching Russian? _No, she isn't._

   b. Does she play the guitar? _Yes, she does._

   c. What is she doing? _She's reading the newspaper._

   d. What does she do for a living? _She teaches Russian._

   e. Does she know Russian grammar? _Yes, she does._

2. a. Does Sally know how to dance? _____

   b. Is she dancing? _____

   c. Is she fixing cars now? _____

   d. What is she doing? _____

   e. What does she do for a living? _____

3. a. Are Isabel and Matt using computers? _____

   b. Do they play chess in their free time? _____

   c. Are they playing chess now? _____

   d. What are they doing? _____

   e. Do they know a lot about computers? _____

4. a. Are you studying English now? _____

   b. Are you studying at home now? _____

   c. Do you usually study in the morning? _____

   d. What do you do in your free time? _____

EXERCISE CONTINUES ▶ ▶

B. Write the questions that go with the answers. Use the words in parentheses.

1. Anne   2. Seth   3. Luke   4. Emily

Job: dentist
Hobby: running

Job: news reporter
Hobby: playing the piano

Job: house husband*
Hobby: computer games

Questions	Answers
1. a. (Anne / do) *What does Anne do (for a living)?*	She's a dentist.
b. (fix teeth) *Is she fixing teeth?*	Yes, she is.
c. (do in her free time) *What does she do in her free time?*	She runs.
d. (run) *Is she running?*	No, she isn't.
2. a. (Seth / do) _____	He's a reporter.
b. (write / a story) _____	No, he isn't.
c. (do) _____	He's playing the piano.
d. (sit) _____	At the piano.
e. (use / a computer for work) _____	Yes, he does.
3. a. (Luke / cook) _____	Yes, he does.
b. (cook) _____	Yes, he is.
c. (play / computer games) _____	Yes, he does
d. (do) _____	He's a house husband*.
4. a. (Emily / laugh) _____	Yes, she is.
b. (eat) _____	No, she isn't.
c. (speak / English) _____	No, she doesn't. She's too young.
d. (look / happy) _____	Yes, she does.

* house husband: *a married man who works at home taking care of the house and children*

UNIT
9

I have . . . and *I've got . . .*

A. Use your own ideas to write sentences with the words in parentheses. Write about yourself, members of your family, or your friends. Use *have/has* or *don't/doesn't have*.

1. (a car) *I have a new car.* OR *I don't have a car.* OR *My friend has a new car.*

2. (a lot of friends) _____

3. (a part-time job) _____

4. (an earache) _____

5. (a lot of free time) _____

B. Use your own ideas to write sentences with the words in parentheses. Use *have/has got* or *haven't/hasn't got*.

1. (a car) *My father has got a car.* OR *I haven't got a car.* _____

2. (a passport) _____

3. (a lot of money) _____

4. (a lot of problems) _____

5. (a fast computer) _____

C. Complete the questions and answers. Use *do, doesn't, don't, got, has, have, hasn't,* or *haven't*.

Questions	Answers
1. Does this house *have* a big back yard?	Yes, it *does* . And the yard is full of trees.
2. _____ Amy got a cold?	No. She _____ got a cold. She has a sore back.
3. Do the Turners _____ a dog?	No, they _____ . But they have a cat.
4. Has your car _____ a big engine?	Yes. It _____ got a very big engine, and it uses a lot of gas.
5. _____ Kim have her own computer?	No, she _____ . She uses her brother's.
6. Have you _____ change for a dollar?	Sorry. I _____ got any change. Ask in the drugstore.

Read the story about a young college woman. Then complete the sentences with the simple present or present continuous of the verbs given.

Sara Mitchell is nineteen years old. She 1) _goes_ (go) to college. She 2) _is_ _studying_ (study) music. She 3) _____ (play) the violin, and she 4) _____ (sing) beautifully. She 5) _____ (study) Spanish, too. She 6) _____ (love) music, but Spanish 7) _____ (seem) very difficult to her. She often 8) _____ (sing) in other languages in her music classes, but usually she 9) _____ (not / understand) the meaning of the words. This year in school she 10) _____ (learn) a different language for the first time. She 11) _____ (need) to learn a lot of new words in Spanish, and she sometimes 12) _____ (forget) the Spanish words in class and on tests.

Sara 13) _____ (have) an apartment near the college with three roommates – Molly, Kate, and Alicia. Sara's roommates 14) _____ (go) to the college too, and Sara 15) _____ (like) them all a lot. They always 16) _____ (do) things together. They often 17) _____ (eat) dinner in the apartment together, and they usually 18) _____ (go) to the movies together on Friday nights. But right now they 19) _____ (not / think) about movies.

Right now Sara 20) _____ (study) for a big Spanish exam. Sara usually 21) _____ (not / do) well on Spanish exams, and she is very worried. Alicia 22) _____ (speak) Spanish well, so she 23) _____ (help) Sara study for the test. Molly and Kate 24) _____ (make) dinner for her. Sara is very lucky to have such nice roommates, and she knows it!

Use your own ideas to write sentences with the words in parentheses. Use the simple present or present continuous.

1. (remember / my first day of school) *I remember my first day of school.*
   OR *My mother doesn't remember my first day of school.*
   _____

2. (listen / to music) *I'm listening to music right now.*
   _____

3. (do / this exercise / on the computer) _____
   _____

4. (play / the guitar) _____
   _____

5. (understand / English grammar) _____
   _____

6. (it / rain / right now) _____
   _____

7. (use / a computer / at work / very often) _____
   _____

8. (it / rain / a lot / here / in the summer) _____
   _____

9. (like / lazy people) _____
   _____

10. (send / e-mail / to my friends / every day) _____
    _____

11. (have got / plans for tonight) _____
    _____

12. (watch / TV / now) _____
    _____

UNITS
10-12

Was/were
Worked, got, went, etc. (Simple Past)
***I didn't . . . Did you . . . ?* (Simple Past Negative and Questions)**

Past

**A. Write two sentences about each picture: a positive one and a negative one.
Use the words in parentheses. Put the verb in the simple past.**

1. *A:* (be / late for school / yesterday)
   Lisa _wasn't late for school yesterday_ .
   B: (get / to school / on time)
   She got to school on time.

2. *A:* (do / his homework / yesterday afternoon)
   Steve _didn't do his homework yesterday afternoon._ .
   B: (play / tennis with a friend)
   He _____ .

3. *A:* (be / tired / Friday night)
   Andrew and Megan _____ .
   B: (go / to the gym)
   They _____ .

4. *A:* (bring / her lunch to work / yesterday)
   Jessica _____ .
   B: (eat / in a restaurant with her friends)
   _____ .

5. *A:* (be / late for work / this morning)
   Martin _____ .
   B: (get up / at 7:30)
   _____ .

6. *A:* (drive / to Miami / last week)
   Nicholas and Rosa _____ .
   B: (fly / first class)
   _____ .

EXERCISE CONTINUES ▶ ▶

B. Now write questions about the people in Part A. Use the words in parentheses. Add any necessary words. Read the answers first.

Questions	Answers
1. (Lisa / get / to school) *What time did Lisa get to school?*	At 8:25.
2. (Steve / do / his homework) When _____ _____ ?	After dinner.
3. (Andrew and Megan / be / tired / last night) Why _____ ?	Because they have difficult jobs.
4. (Jessica's friends / eat) _____ _____	At a Chinese restaurant.
5. (Martin / get up / late / this morning) _____ _____	Because he went to bed late last night.
6. (Nicholas and Rosa / fly / to Miami)_____ _____	Last week.

Was/were
Worked, got, went, etc. (Simple Past)
I didn't . . . Did you . . . ? (Simple Past Negative and Questions)

Complete the paragraphs about getting a driver's license. Use the verbs in the boxes in the simple past.

be	drive	move	~~need~~	want

I 1) *needed* _____ a car when I 2) _____ from Japan to Los Angeles.
After all, public transportation isn't very good in Los Angeles. A person in that city
needs a car to get from home to work and school. At first, my friends in Los Angeles
3) _____ me to work and school. They 4) _____ nice to me,
but I 5) _____ to get a car too. With a car, people have more freedom.
First, I had to get a driver's license.

arrive	be	be	bring	read	learn

I 6) _____ the *California Driver Handbook* to find out about driving in
California. I 7) _____ how to make a left turn correctly and how fast to
drive near a school and on a highway*. The rules 8) _____ new and difficult for
me. The day of my test, a friend 9) _____ me to the place for the driving
test in his car. I 10) _____ very nervous when I 11) _____ there.

be	be	make	pass	take

I 12) _____ two driving tests: a written one and a road test.
Fortunately, I 13) _____ both tests. I 14) _____ surprised
because I think I 15) _____ a mistake during the road test. But the examiner*
16) _____ satisfied* with my driving. I am happy to have my own driver's license.
Now all I need is a car!

* highway: *a wide road where cars can drive fast*
* examiner: *a person who gives a test*
* satisfied: *happy or pleased*

I was doing (Past Continuous)

Complete the conversations with the words in parentheses. Use the past continuous (*was/were + -ing).*

1. *A:* <u>What were you doing</u> (What / you / do) at nine last night?

   B: <u>We were visiting</u> (we / visit) my aunt in the hospital. Why?

   A: I drove by your house, but no one was home.

2. *A:* _____ (you / sleep) at midnight last night?

   B: Yes, I go to bed around 11. Why?

   A: There was a fire at the factory near your house. Didn't you hear the fire trucks?

   B: I think I remember hearing some noise, but I thought _____ (I / dream).

3. *A:* I saw you yesterday. I waved at you, but you didn't see me.

   B: _____ (What / I / do?)

   A: _____ (you / drive) down First Avenue about 10 A.M.

   B: Oh, _____ (I / come) from the dentist. I didn't notice you.

   I guess _____ (I / concentrate*) on driving.

4. *A:* Why _____ (Sue / cry) a little while ago?
   What happened?

   B: _____ (she / not / cry). _____ (she / laugh).
   _____ (some friends / tell) jokes, and she couldn't
   stop laughing.

5. *A:* That was Ellie Bates who _____ (you / talk) to before,
   wasn't it? I didn't know you know her. How did you meet her?

   B: I met her when _____ (I / live) in Washington.
   _____ (she and my wife / work) in the same office.

   * concentrate: *to keep your attention on something*

UNIT
14

I was doing and *I did* (Past Continuous and Simple Past)

**Complete the conversations with the words in parentheses. Use the simple past
or the past continuous.**

1. *A:* _Did you go out for lunch today?_____ (you / go out / for lunch today?)

   B: No, I was in my office at lunchtime. I _was waiting for an important phone call_
   (wait / for an important phone call).

2. *A:* _____ (you / go / out last night?)

   B: No. It _____ (rain).

   We _____ (not / want / to get wet).

3. *A:* I'm sorry I'm late. I _____ (miss) the train.

   It _____ (leave) the station when I _____
   (arrive) at the track.

   B: That's OK. I _____ (finish) my homework while

   I _____ (sit) here.

4. *A:* Were you at home at 7 last night? I _____ (call) you,

   but no one _____ (answer).

   B: I _____ (watch) some music videos at that time. There was

   a lot of noise, so I guess I _____ (not / hear) the phone ring.

5. *A:* How _____ (Tim / hurt / himself)?

   B: He _____ (play / soccer in the park),

   and he _____ (fall).

6. *A:* What _____ (you / do) after the accident

   _____ (happen)?

   B: I _____ (call / the police) on my cell phone.

7. *A:* What _____ (you / do) when the electricity

   _____ (go out)?

   B: I _____ (cook / dinner).

8. *A:* _____ (you / see / John at work today?)

   B: Yes, but we _____ (not / have / time to talk).

I used to . . .

Look at the pictures. They show the people *now*. Use the words in parentheses and *but* to write a sentence about now and the past.

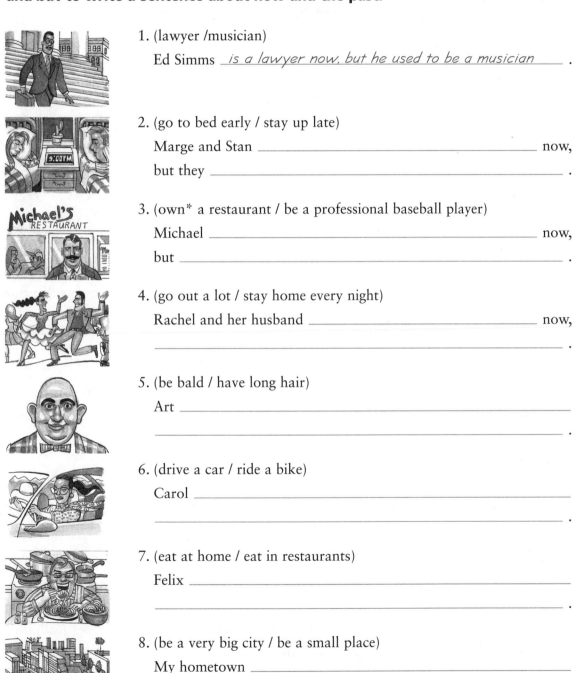

1. (lawyer /musician)

   Ed Simms *is a lawyer now, but he used to be a musician* .

2. (go to bed early / stay up late)

   Marge and Stan _____ now,

   but they _____ .

3. (own* a restaurant / be a professional baseball player)

   Michael _____ now,

   but _____ .

4. (go out a lot / stay home every night)

   Rachel and her husband _____ now,

   _____ .

5. (be bald / have long hair)

   Art _____

   _____ .

6. (drive a car / ride a bike)

   Carol _____

   _____ .

7. (eat at home / eat in restaurants)

   Felix _____

   _____ .

8. (be a very big city / be a small place)

   My hometown _____

   _____ .

* own: *to have something, often a house or a business*

**The police are investigating a break-in* in a neighborhood. They are asking
people questions. Complete the conversation with the simple past or past
continuous of the verbs in parentheses.**

Police officer: **1)** <u>Were you</u> _____ (you / be) at home between four and five
today?

Neighbor: No, I **2)** _____ (be) at work. Why, officer?

Police officer: Someone **3)** _____ (break) into the Brocks' house this afternoon.
4) _____ (anyone else / be) at your house between four and five?

Neighbor: My son **5)** _____ (not / go) to class this afternoon. He's sick. But I
don't think he **6)** _____ (see) anything. I'm sure he **7)** _____
(sleep).

Police officer: What time **8)** _____ (you / come) home from work?

Neighbor: At 5:30, as usual.

Police officer: **9)** _____ (you / see) anything unusual at that time?

Neighbor: Let me think. Now that you ask, I think the Brocks' garage door
10) _____ (be) open. And their dog **11)** _____ (sit) in the
front yard. That was unusual, I guess, but I **12)** _____ (not / think) anything
of it at the time. **13)** _____ (anyone / see) the thieves?

Police officer: No, it seems many of the neighbors **14)** _____ (prepare) dinner,
and others **15)** _____ (watch) the news on TV.

Neighbor: **16)** _____ (the thieves / take) anything?

Police officer: No, it seems that they **17)** _____ (not / know) there was a dog
in the house. I think that they **18)** _____ (look) for money or jewelry and
they were surprised by the dog.

Neighbor: I'm surprised that thieves **19)** _____ (choose) the Brocks' house.
The Brocks are retired*, so they are almost always at home.

Police officer: They **20)** _____ (take) some friends to the airport. When they
21) _____ (get) home around six, they **22)** _____ (call) the police.

Neighbor: Is there anything else I can do for you?

Police officer: No. Thanks, you have been very helpful.

* a break-in: *entering a house by breaking a window or a door to steal things*
* retired: *not working anymore, usually because of age*

Use your own ideas to write sentences with the words in parentheses. Use the simple past, the past continuous, or *used to*. Write positive and negative sentences.

1. (eat / dinner at 7 P.M. last night) _My family ate dinner at 7 P.M. last night._
   (= We sat down and began to eat at 7.)
   OR _My family was eating dinner at 7 P.M. last night._
   (= We started before 7 and the meal was in progress at 7.)
   _____

2. (go / to bed early / when / be / a child) _I used to go to bed early when I was a child._
   _____

3. (sleep / at 2:30 in the morning) _____
   _____

4. (drive / to work last week) _____
   _____

5. (go / to the movies yesterday) _____
   _____

6. (play / soccer / when / be / a child) _____
   _____

7. (stay / home last night) _____
   _____

8. (study / a lot / when / be / in secondary school) _____
   _____

9. (have / an accident when / drive / home the other night) _____
   _____

10. (talk / on the phone at six this morning) _____
    _____

11. (cry / when / hear / the bad news) _____
    _____

Have you ever . . . ? (Present Perfect)

Present Perfect

A. Look at the pictures. Use your own ideas to write sentences in the present perfect with the words in parentheses.

1.   2.   3.   4.

5.   6.   7.   8.

1. (ride a motorcycle) *I've never ridden a motorcycle.* OR *I've ridden a motorcycle once.*

2. (sing in public) _____

3. (drive a truck) _____

4. (eat alone at a restaurant) _____

5. (change a flat tire) _____

6. (cook dinner for ten people) _____

7. (be to Paris) _____

8. (break an arm) _____

B. Now write questions with *ever*. Use the present perfect and the same words in parentheses as in Part A.

1. *Have you ever ridden a motorcycle?*   5. _____

2. Have you ever _____ ?   6. _____

3. _____   7. _____

4. _____   8. _____

EXERCISE 20

How long have you . . . ?

Write questions with *How long has/have* to complete the conversations. Use the present perfect or the present perfect continuous. Look at A's first statement as a clue for which form of the verb to use.

1. *A:* I'm working in a bank now.

   B: How nice. *How long have you been working* there?

   A: For three months.

2. *A:* My father is in Australia on business.

   B: Really? *How long has he been* there?

   A: Since last Monday.

3. *A:* Eric is waiting for a phone call from his uncle.

   B: He is? How long _____ the phone call?

   A: All day.

4. *A:* Did you know that Marcia is a Spanish teacher now?

   B: No. _____ a teacher?

   A: She just started.

5. *A:* My parents are traveling around the country.

   B: Really? _____

   A: For the past two months.

6. *A:* I'm studying Japanese for my trip to Tokyo.

   B: Great. _____ it?

   A: Just a few weeks – this is my first course.

7. *A:* I have a terrible headache.

   B: You poor thing! _____ it?

   A: Since I woke up this morning.

8. *A:* Some good friends of mine live in Hawaii.

   B: Lucky them! _____ there?

   A: They just moved there.

EXERCISE 21

For, since, and *ago*

Answer the questions. Use the words in parentheses and *for, since,* or *ago*.

Questions	Answers
1. Does Martin still live in Seattle?	(go to Africa / a year)
	No, *he went to Africa a year ago* .
2. Does Martin still live in Seattle?	(be in Africa / a year)
	No, *he has been in Africa for a year* .
3. Does Martin still live in Seattle?	(be in Africa / last year)
	No, *he has been in Africa since last year* .
4. Have you had breakfast yet?	(have it / a half hour)
	Yes, I _____ .
5. Is it still raining?	(rain / a long time)
	Yes, it _____ .
6. Do the Lees still live in Philadelphia?	(move to Boston / six months)
	No, they _____ .
7. Is your uncle still in the hospital?	(be there / almost three weeks)
	Yes, _____ .
8. Have you always had dark hair?	(have dark hair / I was little)
	Yes, _____ .
9. Is your headache gone?	(take some aspirin / an hour)
	Yes, _____ .
10. Have your parents been living in Florida long?	(live there / 1982)
	Yes, _____ .
11. Is your son a doctor yet?	(study medicine / three years)
	No, but _____ .
12. Did you meet your husband at work?	(know each other / we were in high school)
	No, _____ .

I have done and *I did* (Present Perfect and Simple Past)
Just, already, and *yet* (Present Perfect and Simple Past)

A. Complete the conversations with the words in parentheses and any other necessary words. Use the present perfect.

1. *A:* Is Andrew Martinez in college?

   B: No, he <u>hasn't finished high school yet</u> (finish / high school / yet).

2. *A:* Would you like some coffee?

   B: No thanks. <u>I've just had some lemonade</u> (just / have / some lemonade).

3. *A:* Are you going to Australia on vacation?

   B: No, we _____ (already / be / there).

4. *A:* I think you should read this book. It's great.

   B: Thanks, but _____ (already / read / it).

5. *A:* _____ (you / see / the boss / yet?)

   B: No, he's been busy all morning.

6. *A:* Are you going to the movies with us?

   B: No, I'm waiting for a phone call, and I _____ (get / it / yet).

7. *A:* _____ (go / to the post office / yet?)

   B: Yeah, why? Do you need something?

B. Complete the conversations with the words in parentheses and any other necessary words. Use the simple past.

1. *A:* Is Carl watching TV?

   B: No, he <u>didn't finish his homework yet</u> (finish / his homework).

2. *A: (on the phone)* You sound strange. What's wrong?

   B: Nothing. I _____ (just / get up).

3. *A:* You need to speak to the boss.

   B: I _____ (already / speak / to her).

4. *A:* I don't think Jeremy knows his mother's in the hospital.

   B: Maybe his father _____ (tell / him / yet).

I've lost my key.
I lost my key last week. (Present Perfect and Simple Past)

Use the words in parentheses to write sentences in the simple past or the present perfect. Some are questions.

1. (my cousin / visit / many countries since he became a pilot) *My cousin has visited many countries since he became a pilot.*

2. (your brother / go / to China last year?) *Did your brother go to China last year?*

3. (my friends / never / eat / Ethiopian food) _____

4. (what time / you / wake up / this morning?) _____

5. (my friend / have / the same job since college) _____

6. (you / ever / be / to Norway?) _____

7. (you / eat / a lot of good food / on your last vacation?) _____

8. (I / not / meet / your parents / until two years ago) _____

9. (you / lose / your wallet at home or at work?) _____

10. (Dean's father / start / his new job / last week) _____

11. (you / ever / stay / at a hotel on the beach?) _____

12. (Janeen / know / her best friend since elementary school) _____

Present Perfect

Use your own ideas to write sentences with the words in parentheses. Use the simple present, simple past, or present perfect.

1. (live / in) *I live in Istanbul.* OR *I've lived in Istanbul since I was born.*
   OR *I didn't live in Istanbul from 1999 to 2001.*

2. (know / my best friend / since) _____

3. (have / the same hairstyle / for) _____

4. (buy / something expensive / ago) _____

5. (never / see / before) _____

6. (be / Australia) _____

7. (life / change / a lot) _____

8. (not / do / yet) _____

9. (take / last year) _____

10. (be / sick / a few days) _____

11. (work / for the same company / a long time) _____

12. (just / remember) _____

13. (go / to bed / last night) _____

14. (live / in many places) _____

15. (already / eat) _____

U N I T
22

Is done and *was done* (Passive)

Passive

Use the words in parentheses to write sentences in the passive (present or past). Some are questions.

1. *A:* This city is very crowded.
   B: (more houses / build / every year) Yes. *More houses are built every year.*

2. *A:* Did you do well on your exam?
   B: (we / not / give / enough time) No. *We weren't given enough time.*

3. *A:* Why didn't you receive your phone bills?
   B: (they / sent / to my old address) _____

4. This plant is very rare. (it / find / in only a few places) _____
   _____

5. *A:* Is soccer popular in Canada?
   B: (it / not / play much / twenty years ago) _____
   _____ However, it is very popular now.

6. (oil / not / import / by Venezuela) _____
   The country produces a lot of oil and exports it.

7. Someone broke into your house? (anything / steal?) _____

8. *A:* (anyone / injure / in the accident?) _____
   B: Yes, unfortunately. (two people / take / to the hospital) _____
   _____

9. *A:* (how many people / need / to make a basketball team?) _____
   _____
   B: There are five on each team.

10. *A:* What are those flowers?
    B: (they / call / "daffodils") _____

11. *A:* (when / this package / deliver / here?) _____
    B: I don't know for sure. Sometime this morning, I think.

Is done and *was done* (Passive)
Is being done and *has been done* (Passive)

Put a check (✔) next to the sentence that is similar in meaning to the first.

1. Ken's bicycle was hit by a car.

   _____ a. A driver was hit by Ken's bicycle.

   __✔__ b. A car hit Ken's bicycle.

   _____ c. Ken hit a car with his bicycle.

2. Patients are given everything they need in the hospital.

   _____ a. Patients don't need anything in the hospital.

   _____ b. Hospitals give patients what they need.

   _____ c. Patients need a lot of things.

3. I can't lend you my jacket. It's being cleaned.

   _____ a. My jacket's dirty, so you don't want to wear it.

   _____ b. I'm going to clean my jacket, so I can't give it to you.

   _____ c. I've taken my jacket to the cleaner's, and so I can't lend it to you.

4. Am I being told the truth?

   _____ a. Are people telling me the truth?

   _____ b. Am I telling the truth?

   _____ c. Am I telling a lie?

5. Has the position* been filled?

   _____ a. Are you filling that position?

   _____ b. Have you hired* someone?

   _____ c. Have you fired* someone?

6. At a potluck meal, everyone who is invited brings something to eat or drink.

   _____ a. The people who invite others to a potluck meal buy all the food and drinks.

   _____ b. Food and drinks are brought by the people who are invited to a potluck meal.

   _____ c. The guests at a potluck meal don't prepare any food.

7. The electric bill hasn't been paid.

   _____ a. We don't need to pay the electric bill.

   _____ b. Someone has paid the electric bill.

   _____ c. No one has paid the electric bill.

8. Are you being helped?

   _____ a. Is someone helping you?

   _____ b. Did you give someone help?

   _____ c. Are you helping someone?

9. The tree was cut down after it was damaged in a storm.

   _____ a. The tree fell down during the storm.

   _____ b. People cut down the tree after the storm damaged it.

   _____ c. People cut down the tree because it caused a lot of damage.

* position: *a job*
* hire: *to give someone a job*
* fire: *to remove someone from a job, e.g., He was fired for stealing.*

Is done and *was done* (Passive)
Is being done and *has been done* (Passive)

Write answers to the questions in the passive. Use the same verb and tense used in the question.

Questions	Answers
1. Do they grow rice in Alaska?	No, rice _is grown_ in warm, wet places.
2. Who invited you to the party?	_We were invited_ by Thomas.
3. Have they fixed your computer yet?	Yes, it _has been fixed_ already.
4. Did Einstein invent the electric light?	No, it _____ _____ by Thomas Edison.
5. How often do the companies send electric and water bills?	The bills _____ _____ every month.
6. Do they check every bag at airport security?	No, but many bags _____ _____ by security.
7. Did your son break your window?	No, it _____ _____ by another boy.
8. Is the town building a new hospital?	Yes, it _____ _____ close to here.
9. Are you using this computer?	No, but I think that _____ _____ by someone else.
10. Do they sell lottery tickets everywhere?	No, _____ _____ only at certain stores.
11. Did you cut down those trees yourself?	No, _____ _____ by a tree service.
12. *(at a hotel)* Has anyone cleaned your room yet?	Yes, it _____ _____ already.
13. *(in a store)* Is anyone helping you?	Yes, thanks, I _____ _____ .
14. Who is taking care of your children tonight?	_____ _____ by their grandmother.

REVIEW
Passive

Use your own ideas to write sentences in the passive with the words in parentheses. Use an appropriate form of the verb, and add any necessary words.

1. (building / build) _A large apartment building is being built across from the school._

2. (languages / speak) _____

3. (a good program / show) _____

4. (my favorite dish / make) _____

5. (computer / repair) _____

6. (invite / to a lot of parties) _____

7. (buildings / destroy / in the earthquake) _____

8. (music / play) _____

9. (some children / name) _____

10. (a new drug / develop) _____

Be, have, and do in Present and Past Tenses

Verb Forms

**Complete the conversations with *am/is/are, was/were, do/does, did,* or *has/have.*
Use *not* if necessary. Some sentences are active, and some are passive.**

1. *A:* _Did_____ Karen call you last night?

   B: _Are_____ you serious? Karen _hasn't_____ called me for months and months.

2. *A:* _____ your jacket from Scotland?

   B: No, I think it _____ made in China, actually.

3. *A:* My brother likes his job, but he _____ like the hours.

   B: What hours _____ he work?

   A: Usually from 10 A.M. to 7 P.M., but he _____ come home until 9:30 last night.

4. *A:* I think I _____ lost my watch. _____ you seen it anywhere?

   B: No. _____ you leave it in the bathroom?

   A: No. I _____ already looked there.

   B: _____ you check your pockets?

   A: Of course.

5. *A:* _____ it raining when you left for work this morning?

   B: No. That's why I _____ take my umbrella with me this morning. Now it
   _____ raining and I really need it.

6. *A:* _____ you return my book to the library this morning?

   B: No, I _____ left the house all day. _____ you ask me to return it?

   A: I left you a note, but I guess you _____ see it.

   B: Sorry. Where _____ you leave it?

   A: On the refrigerator.

7. *A:* *(in a store)* _____ you been helped?

   B: Actually, I _____ just looking, thanks. But I have a question.

   A: Yes?

   B: _____ these pants and jackets sold together or separately?

   A: Separately.

   B: That's what I thought. Thanks.

UNITS
24-25

Be, have, and do in Present and Past Tenses
Regular and Irregular Verbs

A. Complete these questions about a friend's new computer. Use is/are, was/were, do/does, did, or has/have.

1. _Did_ _____ you buy your computer at a store or directly from the company?

2. How long _____ you had your new computer?

3. Where _____ your computer made?

4. _____ you use it for work or for personal business?

5. _____ it have a lot of memory?

6. _____ you taken any computer courses?

7. _____ you thinking of getting a new printer, too?

8. _____ you also buy the desk that the computer is on?

9. _____ your computer used by other people in your family?

B. Now complete answers to the questions in Part A. Use the correct form (past tense or past participle) of the verb in parentheses.

1. I _bought_ _____ (buy) it at a local store.

2. I _____ (get) it a month ago.

3. It's American, but some of the parts _____ (come) from Mexico.

4. So far, I've _____ (use) it just for work.

5. I have never _____ (understand) computer memory, but it's a fast computer.

6. Yes, I _____ (take) a class last spring.

7. Yes, I have to because my old one _____ (break).

8. No, I _____ (find) an old desk in the basement.

9. Yes, it is _____ (use) by my children to do their homework.

EXERCISE 31

What are you doing tomorrow?

Pam is a salesperson for a computer company. She has to go to Denver next week. Look at her calendar. Use the words in parentheses to write sentences about her schedule. Use the simple present or the present continuous to tell about the future.

MONDAY	TUESDAY	WEDNESDAY
Flight to Denver: 7:50 A.M. Arrive at 9:15	9 A.M.: Meeting at Best Computer Services	Return flight to Atlanta: 6:35 A.M.
Get bus for downtown: 9:30	12:30: Lunch with my college friend Kate	Arrive Atlanta: 10:15 A.M.
11 A.M. – 5 P.M.: Work in office. Look at our company's new products; discuss products with other salespeople.	3 P.M.: Deliver and explain new computer design to City Hospital downtown	Bus from airport at 11 A.M. Take the rest of the day off*!
Go to hotel	6 P.M.: Dinner and *Hamlet* with my in-laws*. Play at 8.	

1. (fly / Denver / on Monday) *Pam is flying to Denver on Monday.*

2. (her flight to Denver / leave / at 7:50 A.M.) *Her flight to Denver leaves at 7:50 A.M.*

3. (discuss / her company's new products / in the afternoon) She _____ .

4. (not / stay / with relatives / in Denver) _____

5. (Tuesday / have / lunch / college friend) _____

6. (in the evening / go out / her in-laws) _____

* in-laws: *your husband's or wife's relatives, such as his or her parents*
* take a day off: *not to work that day*

EXERCISE CONTINUES ▶ ▶

7. (they / see / a play) _____

_____

8. (play / begin / 8) _____

_____

9. (her flight / on Wednesday / leave / very early) _____

_____

10. (return / to Atlanta / on Wednesday) _____

_____

11. (husband / not / meet / her at the airport) _____

_____

12. (her bus / depart / from the airport / at 11 A.M.) _____

_____

13. (not / go / the office / on Wednesday) _____

_____

I'm going to . . .
Will

Ms. Jenkins's class is always ready to help. Use the words in parentheses, and write (a) what Ms. Jenkins says about her *plans* for the class and (b) what the students say to *offer* help. Use *going to* for plans and *will* for offers.

1. *a.* (we / take a trip to the nature center)

    Ms. Jenkins: <u>We're going to take a trip to the nature center.</u>

    b. (bring / my camera)

    Ben: <u>I'll bring my camera.</u>

2. *a.* (study / Native Americans / in April)

    Ms. Jenkins: We are _____.

    b. (bring / pictures of our family trip to Arizona)

    Barbara: I _____.

3. *a.* (plant / a garden in the school yard in the spring)

    Ms. Jenkins: _____

    b. (bring / some seeds from home)

    Andrew and Lisa: We _____.

4. *a.* (have / party / next month)

    Ms. Jenkins: _____

    b. (my mother / make cookies / us)

    Elizabeth: _____

Use your own ideas to write sentences. Look at the words in parentheses and discuss your plans or decisions in a sentence with *going to*. Then tell more about your plans or decisions in a sentence with *I think I will* or *I don't think I will*.

1. (buy a new car next year) *I'm not going to buy a new car next year. I don't think I will have enough money.* OR *I think I will wait for another year or two.*

2. (take a trip to Hawaii next winter) _____

3. (change jobs soon) _____

4. (take an aerobics class next month) _____

5. (visit relatives in the next two or three months) _____

6. (get some new clothes soon) _____

7. (spend a lot of money this coming year) _____

8. (move to another city in a few months) _____

Rewrite the sentences. Use *might* instead of *maybe* or *perhaps*.

1. Perhaps Jason is sick again.
   Jason might be sick again.

2. Maybe we won't see you tomorrow.
   We might not see you tomorrow.

3. Maybe Nicole will be in town next week.
   Nicole might _____ .

4. Perhaps it will rain tomorrow.
   It _____ .

5. Maybe the driver doesn't know the way to our house.

   _____

6. Maybe Manuel will forget to call us.

   _____

7. Perhaps we'll go to Central America for vacation.

   _____

8. Maybe my friends will do volunteer work* this weekend.

   _____

9. Maybe you have a cold.

   _____

10. Perhaps James won't be on time for work tomorrow.

    _____

11. Maybe I'll watch TV tonight.

    _____

12. Perhaps we won't recognize Uncle Joe when we see him.

    _____

* volunteer work: *work that is not paid and that usually is done to help other people in the community*

Can and *could*

Complete the sentences with *can('t)* or *could(n't)* and one of the verbs in the box.

~~come~~	decide	find	get	play	read
sleep	speak	~~swim~~	use	~~write~~	

1. _Could_ OR _Can_ you _write_ your address down for me, please?

2. I never go to the ocean with my friends because I _can't swim_ .

3. I heard your party was a lot of fun. I'm sorry we _couldn't come_ .

4. _____ I _____ your cell phone to make a call?

5. I'm looking for some sugar for my coffee, but I _____ any.

6. _____ you _____ some sugar at the store?
   We need some.

7. Hannah wanted to buy a new dress last night, but she _____ which
   one she liked better.

8. I think I'll enjoy my trip to Japan because I _____ a little Japanese.

9. Melissa's very smart. When she was four, she _____ already
   _____ some words in her children's books.

10. Brandon is very good at sports. He _____ soccer, football, baseball,
    and tennis well.

11. My apartment building was very noisy last night. I _____ .

EXERCISE 36

Must

Complete the sentences with *must* or *must not* and one of the phrases in the box.

be tired	be upset	be vegetarians*	drink coffee	feel well today
have children	have enough money	know him	know it very well	like rice

1. Juan never goes out to eat with us. He *must not have enough money* .

2. You worked 12 hours today? You *must be tired* .

3. Sylvia never eats rice, even when we go to a Chinese restaurant. She _____

    _____ .

4. The Rileys have only lived in Miami a few weeks. They _____ .

5. Pete always orders juice or a soda when we go out. He _____ .

6. Jenny and Michael never order meat when we eat out. They _____ .

7. That actor is very famous. You _____ .

8. I saw small bikes and toys outside our new neighbors' house. They _____

    _____ .

9. Ryan's car broke down* again. He _____ .

10. Ellen's usually so friendly, but she's not today. She _____ .

    * vegetarian: *a person who does not eat meat*
    * break down: *to stop working*

Should

**Look at the pictures. Write a sentence for each picture with *I think . . . should*
or *I don't think . . . should* and the correct phrase from the box.**

1.   2.   3.   4.

5.   6.   7.   8.

drive more carefully	ask for help to fix her flat tire	go for a walk right now
go to work today	make noise near a hospital	watch TV for such a long time
~~swim here~~	use her phone while she is driving	

1. I don't think he   *should swim here*   .

2. I don't think they _____ .

3. _____

4. _____

5. _____

6. _____

7. _____

8. _____

A. Rewrite the sentences with a form of *have to*. Keep the same meaning.

1. It is necessary to pay in order to park in this lot.

   You _have to pay to park in this lot_ .

2. It is not necessary for passengers in the backseat to wear seat belts.

   Passengers in the backseat don't have to wear seat belts.

3. Is it necessary for me to take a driving test to get a license?

   Do I have to take a driving test to get a license?

4. Is it necessary for drivers to have insurance in this state?

   _____

5. It is not necessary for tourists to have a local driver's license in many places.

   _____

6. It is necessary for drivers to wear seat belts.

   _____

B. Rewrite the sentences with *must* or *must not*. (Note: you *are required* to do something = you *must* do it; you *are forbidden* to do something = you *must not* do it.)

1. You are required to have a credit card to rent a car.

   You _must have a credit card to rent a car_ .

2. You are forbidden to take pictures in the museum.

   You _must not take pictures in the museum_ .

3. Swimmers are required to take a shower before going into the pool.

   Swimmers _____ .

4. It is forbidden to park your car in front of the fire station.

   You _____ .

5. Smoking is forbidden in this building.

   You _____ .

EXERCISE 39

Would you like . . . ? I'd like . . .

Complete the conversations. Use *like* or *would like*. Use the words in parentheses and any other necessary words.

1. *A:* (what / you / like / for dinner) *What would you like for dinner?* _____ Pasta?

   B: (not / like / pasta very much) No, I *don't like pasta very much* _____ .

   A: How about fish?

   B: (like / fish a lot) Yes, I *like fish a lot* _____ .

2. *A:* (you / like / your Spanish class?) _____

   B: Yes, my teacher is great.

3. *A:* (like / buy / Gary a present) I _____ .
      It's his birthday.

   B: What are going to buy for him?

   A: A CD or maybe a DVD. (like / music a lot) He _____ .

4. *A:* (what / you / like / drink?) _____

   B: Iced tea if you have any.

   A: All right. (you / like / sugar in it?) _____

   B: No, thanks.

5. *A:* (you / like / foreign movies?) _____

   B: Yes, usually. Is there one playing?

   A: Yes, a Spanish film. (you / like / go / tonight?) _____

   _____

   B: Sure. What time?

Would you like . . . ? I'd like . . .
I'd rather . . .

Complete the conversations with the words in parentheses and any other necessary ones.

1. *A:* Would you rather go shopping or stay home tonight?

   B: I have another idea. (like / go / the movies) I <u>'d like to go to the movies</u> .

   A: (rather / stay / home) I <u>'d rather stay home</u> . Let's rent a video.

2. *A:* (where / you / like / sit?) _____

   B: Near the front if it's OK with you.

3. *A:* Shall I tell Ana about the accident, or would you like to tell her?

   B: (rather / not / tell / her) I _____ . You do it.

4. *A:* (what / you / like / have / for dessert?) _____

   B: I think I'll just have some coffee, please.

5. *A:* Would your sister like to be a doctor?

   B: (rather / be / a teacher) Actually, she _____ .

6. *A:* Are your brother and his wife excited about moving to New York?

   B: (rather / not / move there) No, actually they _____ .
   They like Seattle.

7. *A:* Have you heard about Justin's problem?

   B: Yes. (not / like / be / in his position) I _____ .

8. *A:* Is your daughter going to go to a large college?

   B: No. (rather / go / to a small college / a large one) She _____
   _____ .

9. *A:* Shall we eat at home tonight?

   B: No. (rather / go out / eat at home) I _____ .

Do this! Don't do that! Let's do this!

Write sentences with the words in parentheses to respond to the suggestions. Make the first sentence positive and the second sentence negative. Use the base form or *Let's (not)* in the responses.

1. *A:* What shall we have for dessert?
   B: (ice cream) *Let's have ice cream.*
   (chocolate cake again) *Let's not have chocolate cake again.*

2. *A:* What should I make for dinner?
   B: (fish) *Make fish.*
   (chicken again) *Don't make chicken again.*

3. *A:* When should I pay the bills?
   B: (next week) _____
   (this week) _____

4. *A:* What should I wear to the party?
   B: (a suit and tie) _____
   (your old tennis shoes) _____

5. *A:* Whose relatives should we invite?
   B: (my relatives) _____
   (your relatives) _____

6. *A:* What should I get at the store?
   B: (some fruit and yogurt) _____
   (any cookies this time) _____

7. *A:* Where shall we go for dinner?
   B: (a new restaurant) _____
   (the same old place) _____

8. *A:* Where do you want to go for vacation?
   B: (Montreal this time) _____
   (Alaska again) _____

You are asking Michelle about her plans. Look at the questions and answers. Then complete the list of Michelle's plans. Use *can('t)* or *might (not)* where possible.

Your questions	Michelle's answers
1. Do you want to play tennis with us tomorrow?	Sorry, I don't have time.
2. Are you going out tonight?	Yes, I am.
3. Are you working this weekend?	I'm not sure.
4. Can you help us move on Saturday?	Yes, you can count on* me.
5. Are you going to watch the game on TV Sunday?	Yes! Definitely!*
6. Are you planting a garden next spring?	Maybe.
7. Will you be at home tomorrow night?	No, I won't.
8. Would you like to play chess this afternoon?	I'm working this afternoon.
9. Are you going to Colombia next summer?	It depends on money.
10. Are you going shopping with us on Thursday?	Sorry, I'm busy on Thursday.

List of Michelle's Plans

1. *Michelle can't play tennis with us tomorrow.*
2. *She is going out tonight.*
3. *She might work this weekend.*
4. She _____ .
5. _____
6. _____
7. _____
8. _____
9. _____
10. _____

* count on (someone): *to depend on someone*
* definitely: *for sure*

Look at the picture of a movie theater. Complete the sentences with *might*, *can/could*, *must*, *should*, *have to*, or *would like/rather* and the words in parentheses. In some cases, more than one verb is correct.

A MOVIE THEATER

1. The teenagers <u>*should put*</u> (put) their feet on the floor.

2. The teenagers <u>*shouldn't have*</u> (not / have) their feet on the seats.

3. The little boy _____ (like) popcorn a lot.

4. The little girl's soda _____ (fall).

5. The little girl _____ (eat) some of the little boy's popcorn.

6. This movie theater has a rule: People _____ (turn off) their cell phones. They _____ (not / use) cell phones anywhere in the theater.

7. The man _____ (not / talk) on his cell phone during the movie.

8. One woman is covering her face because she doesn't want to look at the movie. The movie _____ (be) scary.

EXERCISE CONTINUES ▶ ▶

9. A man is sleeping. He _____ (be) tired. He
   _____ (not / stay awake).

10. A man is sitting behind a man with a cowboy hat. He _____
    (not / see) the movie very well. He _____ (move) to another
    seat.

11. A man and his wife haven't sat down yet. They _____ (not /
    agree) about where to sit. Some people like to sit in the front of the theater, but other
    people _____ (sit) near the back.

12. The man with the cap is looking for someone. He _____ (have)
    a friend in the audience.

13. There aren't many people in the theater. The movie _____
    (not / be) very popular.

Modals, Imperatives, etc.

Use your own ideas to complete the sentences.

1. Some people can't _drive_ OR _speak a foreign language_ OR _cook very well_ .
   Some people can't _____ .

2. As a child, I could(n't) _____ .

3. On weekends, I sometimes have to _____ .

4. I don't have to _____ this weekend, however.

5. I think parents should _____ .

6. But I don't think parents should _____ .

7. Not many people would like _____ .

8. I would rather _____ than _____ .

9. Some drivers have a lot of accidents. They must _____ .

10. In five years, the world might _____ .

11. I would not like _____ . I would rather _____
    _____ .

12. People who can't _____ should not _____
    _____ .

13. Some people make a lot of mistakes. They must not _____
    _____ .

14. If someone _____ , we might not _____ .

15. Some people would rather not _____ unless it is necessary.

There is / are

Look at the picture of the house. The information in the sentences doesn't match the picture. Rewrite each sentence to correct it.

1. There's a car in the driveway.
   There are two cars in the driveway.

2. There is a dog in the yard.
   There isn't a dog in the yard.

3. There are no mailboxes on this street.

   _____

4. There's a cat in the window.

   _____

5. There are two flower gardens in the front yard.

   _____

EXERCISE CONTINUES ▶ ▶

There and It (vertical text, left margin)

6. There isn't any grass in the yard.

_____

7. There are some trees in the yard.

_____

8. There's a truck in front of the house.

_____

9. There isn't a garage behind the house.

_____

10. There are no police in the neighborhood now.

_____

11. There's a bird on the chimney.

_____

12. There's a chair in the yard.

_____

13. There are two bikes against the house.

_____

14. There is a child in the yard.

_____

There is/are
There was/were there will be there has been / have been

Complete the sentence in column B so that it has the same meaning as the sentence in column A. Use *there* in your sentences.

A	**B**
1. It isn't cloudy today.	*There aren't* _____ clouds in the sky today.
2. Did someone rob the bank?	*Was there* _____ a robbery at the bank?
3. This dessert is very sweet.	_____ a lot of sugar in the dessert.
4. My old high school has changed a lot.	_____ a lot of changes in my old high school.
5. It will be very windy this afternoon.	_____ strong winds this afternoon.
6. I couldn't sleep because it was too noisy.	I couldn't sleep because _____ too much noise.
7. A lot of people came to the meeting.	_____ a lot of people at the meeting.
8. Ice cream is a very fattening food*.	_____ a lot of fat and sugar in ice cream.
9. It has rained heavily all day.	_____ heavy rain all day.
10. I don't have any reason to go to the store. I have all the things I need right now.	_____ no reason for me to go to the store.
11. We will have to wait for the plane to arrive.	_____ a delay in the arrival of the plane.
12. The people in the next room are having a party.	_____ a party in the next room.
13. This computer had some problems.	_____ some problems with this computer.

* fattening food: *a food that makes people fat when they eat a lot of it*

There is/are
There was/were there will be there has been / have been
It . . .

Write B's answers to A's questions and statements. Use the words in parentheses. Use *it* or *there* + the verb *be* in an appropriate form.

1. *A:* How's the weather today?
   B: (a lot of wind) *There's a lot of wind.*

2. *A:* Why did it take so long to do the shopping?
   B: (a lot of people at the store) *There were a lot of people at the store.*

3. *A:* How was your flight?
   B: (long but good) *It was long but good.*

4. *A:* How's the weather today?
   B: (windy) _____

5. *A:* Is Los Angeles far from here?
   B: (almost 500 miles) _____ from here.

6. *A:* Did you enjoy your walk last night?
   B: (dark and cold) No, _____ .

7. *A:* Have you been to Denver?
   B: (a big conference there last year) Yes, _____ .

8. *A:* Did you have a good trip?
   B: (a lot of traffic on the highway) Yes, but _____ .

9. *A:* Why aren't you drinking your coffee? Isn't it good?
   B: (not hot enough) Yes, but _____ .

10. *A:* Did you take the train home last night?
    B: (a train at 9:30) Yes, _____ .

11. *A:* I'm sorry you got to the game late.
    B: I am, too. (difficult to find a parking space) _____

12. *A:* Was the movie crowded?
    B: (not many people in the ticket line) No, _____ .

UNIT
41

I am, I don't, etc.

Auxiliary Verbs

A. Answer these questions about yourself. Use *Yes, I do; No, I'm not*, etc.

1. Can you speak Chinese?   *No, I can't.* OR *Yes, I can.*
2. Have you ever been to Egypt?   *Yes, I have.* OR *No, I haven't.*
3. Do you have many relatives? _____
4. Will you be at home Saturday night? _____
5. Were you at home this morning? _____
6. Did you go out last night? _____
7. Are you working tomorrow? _____
8. Was the weather in your town nice yesterday? _____
9. Are there many parks in your town? _____
10. Have you ever eaten Thai food? _____

B. Complete the sentences with an auxiliary verb, positive or negative.

1. I feel fine today, but I _didn't_ yesterday.

2. I don't have a car, but my brother _does_ .

3. *A:* Have you eaten lunch yet?
   B: I have, but my friend _____ .

4. My best friend likes hot weather, but I _____ .

5. It didn't rain yesterday, but it _____ the day before.

6. I like living in Florida, but my family _____ .

7. My wife is from a small town, but I _____ .

8. *A:* Are you going to do your homework this afternoon?
   B: I should, but I probably _____ .

9. I've never been to India, but my parents _____ .

10. *A:* Is it going to rain today?
    B: It _____ . I don't know.

You have? / have you?   you are? / are you?, etc.
Too/either and so am I / neither do I, etc.

Read the statement in the first column. Write a short question to show interest, in the second column. Then indicate that the same is true for you by writing *So do I, Neither did I*, etc. in the third column.

A friend's statement	Your short question	So / Neither . . .
1. I feel a little tired today.	*You do?*	*So do I.*
2. My sister just got married.	*She did?*	*So did I.*
3. I have never been to New York City.	*You haven't?*	*Neither have I.*
4. I stayed home last night.		
5. I'm not going to work tomorrow.		
6. I can't understand Brandon.		
7. I'll be late for work tomorrow.		
8. I'm not from Sydney.		
9. I don't like coffee very much.		
10. I've been tired lately.		
11. I'd like to take a break now.		
12. Nick couldn't go to Laurie's party.		
13. My parents don't watch much TV.		
14. My brother is very good at computers.		

Complete the sentences with a tag question. Then choose an answer from the list below.

Questions		Answers
1. Those aren't grapes, *are they*	?	*d*
2. Vicky was at work yesterday, *wasn't she*	?	*f*
3. You don't eat meat, _____	?	___
4. You'll come to our party, _____	?	___
5. There aren't any messages for me, _____	?	___
6. You haven't forgotten my birthday, _____	?	___
7. Lisa called you, _____	?	___
8. You're not too tired to go to the movies, _____	?	___
9. You don't like ice cream, _____	?	___
10. You're going to work tomorrow, _____	?	___
11. You were sick yesterday, _____	?	___
12. Your parents aren't Mexican, _____	?	___

Answers

  a. Yes, she did. Why?

  b. No, I'm a vegetarian*.

  c. No, I want to go.

✓d. No, they're cherries.

  e. No, they're Chilean.

✓f. Yes, I'm sure I saw her.

  g. Yes, I don't like to miss work.

  h. Yes, but I'm better now.

  i. Not especially. Do you have something else?

  j. Yes. Can I bring something?

  k. Of course not. I have a present for you.

  l. No. No one called today.

   * vegetarian: *a person who does not eat meat*

UNIT
44

Isn't . . . , haven't . . . , don't . . . , etc. (Negatives)

Rewrite the sentences so that they make sense*. Change verbs to the negative where necessary.

1. Paulo likes his boss because she isn't very nice to him.

   Paulo doesn't like his boss because she isn't very nice to him.

2. The world needs another war; it needs more peace.

   The world doesn't need another war; it needs more peace.

3. I go to bed early when I'm not sleepy.

   _____

4. Fish have wings, but birds do.

   _____

5. Read that book if you don't find it interesting.

   _____

6. You should work extra hours if you don't feel well.

   _____

7. I walked to school because the buses were running because of bad weather.

   _____

8. We ate the fish because it didn't smell very good to us.

   _____

9. They study very hard, so they don't get very good grades.

   _____

10. Sheila was here yesterday, so she didn't hear the news.

    _____

11. I'll see you tomorrow if you can't be here.

    _____

* make sense: *to be understandable, to be logical*

Too / either and *so am I / neither do I,* etc.
Isn't . . . , haven't . . . , don't . . . , etc. (Negatives)

Complete the sentences with the words in parentheses. Use an appropriate form of the verb.

1. (I / study / last night) _I didn't study last night_ , and neither did my friend.

2. (my son / have / a headache) _My son has a headache_ , and so do I.

3. (my boss / be / to Canada) _____ , and neither have I.

4. (my brother / fix a car) _____ , and I can too.

5. (the Mendozas / from Mexico) _____ , and neither are the Carrillos.

6. (my car / be / for sale) _____ , and neither is my neighbor's.

7. (I / catch / the flu last year) _____ , and so did everyone else in my office.

8. (I / watch the news last night) _____ , and my wife didn't either.

9. (my father / like / his job) _____ , and neither does my brother.

10. (Tony / do / his homework now) _____ , and Julia isn't either.

11. (Edgar / be / born / in Canada) _____ , and so were his parents.

12. (I / be / at work tomorrow) _____ , and the boss won't either.

13. (I / work / a little harder) _____ , and so should you.

14. (I / like / to live in a big city) _____ , and my family wouldn't either.

EXERCISE 53

REVIEW

Auxiliary Verbs

Complete the sentences about yourself and people you know.

1. *My friends don't get up early* _____ , but I do.

   My neighbor doesn't have a car _____ , but I do.

   My sister doesn't teach children _____ , but I do.

   _____ , but I do.

2. A friend of mine used to work in a bank, *and I did too* OR *and so did I* OR *but I didn't* _____ .

   A friend of mine used to work in a bank, _____ .

3. _____ , and so does my friend.

4. _____ , and so am I.

5. _____ , but I did.

6. Some people don't like dogs, _____ .

7. _____ , but I haven't.

8. _____ , but someone might.

9. Many people have musical talent, _____ .

10. _____ , and so will I.

11. _____ , and neither has my friend.

12. _____ , but a few have.

13. _____ , but she said she was going to.

14. Most people that I know don't like to work, _____ .

15. _____ , but I wouldn't.

16. Some people are not good writers, _____ .

17. _____ , and so did I.

UNIT
45

Questions

Is it . . . ?, Have you . . . ?, Do they . . . ?, etc.

Your friend is taking a trip. Complete the questions.

Your friend says:	You ask:
1. We're going to Hawaii.	When _are you going_ ?
2. We would like to visit more than one island there.	Which islands _____ ?
3. I've bought some things for the trip.	What things _____ ?
4. Our plane leaves very early.	What time _____ ?
5. It takes a long time to fly to Hawaii.	How long _____ ?
6. The tickets didn't cost very much.	How much _____ ?
7. I haven't told my parents about the trip.	Why _____ ?
8. We take a few trips every year.	How many _____ ?
9. We went to Puerto Rico recently.	When _____ ?
10. We also traveled someplace else a few months ago.	Where _____ ?
11. We were planning to go to Mexico.	Where in Mexico _____ ?
12. We changed our minds about going there.	Why _____ ?
13. We've been there before.	How many times _____ ?
14. We go there often.	How often _____ ?
15. I have a lot of vacation time.	How much _____ ?

Who saw you? Who did you see?

Write questions. Ask about the underlined word.

Statements	Questions
1. <u>SOMEONE</u> is getting married next week.	Who _is getting married next week_ ?
2. I called <u>SOMEONE</u> last night.	Who _did you call last night_ ?
3. I saw <u>SOMETHING</u>.	What _____ ?
4. <u>SOMETHING</u> is happening.	What _____ ?
5. <u>SOMETHING</u> happened to me yesterday.	What _____ ?
6. <u>SOMEONE</u> lives in a castle.	Who _____ ?
7. My neighbors have <u>SOMETHING</u>.	What _____ ?
8. <u>SOMETHING</u> woke me up this morning.	What _____ ?
9. I eat <u>SOMETHING</u> for breakfast every morning.	What _____ ?
10. I know <u>SOMEONE</u>.	Who _____ ?
11. <u>SOMEONE</u> teaches physics.	Who _____ ?
12. I asked <u>SOMEONE</u> for directions.	Who _____ ?
13. <u>SOMEONE</u> fixed the broken window.	Who _____ ?
14. We need <u>SOMETHING</u> for the recipe.	What _____ ?
15. <u>SOMETHING</u> surprised us yesterday.	What _____ ?

Who is she talking to? What is it like?

A. Complete the conversations with the verb in parentheses and a preposition. Use any other necessary words.

1. *A:* Mary Jo is talking on the phone again!

   B: Who _is she talking to_ _____ (talk)?

   A: I don't know.

2. *A:* What are you doing?

   B: Waiting.

   A: What _____ (wait)?

   B: For the mail.

3. *A:* Are these your books?

   B: No, they're not.

   A: Who _____ (belong)?

   B: To that man over there, I think.

4. *A:* Are you busy?

   B: Yes, I'm writing a letter.

   A: Who _____ (write)?

   B: To a friend from school.

5. *A:* Can I borrow your dictionary?

   B: Sorry, I don't have it. I lent it to someone.

   A: Who _____ (lend)?

   B: To my brother.

6. *A:* How was your trip?

   B: Great. We loved our hotel.

   A: Which _____ (stay)?

   B: At the Biltmore.

7. *A:* I saw a great old movie last night.

   B: What _____ (be)?

   A: It was about a bank robbery.

EXERCISE CONTINUES ▶ ▶

8. *A:* I don't understand how you can travel alone.

   B: I'm not traveling alone.

   A: Oh? Who _____ (travel)?

   B: With my cousin.

B. Now write questions with *What is/are . . . like?* or *What was/were . . . like?*

1. *A:* We have some new neighbors.

   B: _What are they like?_ _____ (they)

   A: They seem friendly.

2. *A:* We went to the beach in Florida.

   B: _What was the water like?_ _____ (the water)

   A: Warm and wonderful.

3. *A:* We drove on the freeways of Los Angeles last week.

   B: Really? _____ (the traffic)

   A: It was scary*. The cars move really fast.

4. *A:* I finally met my wife's family.

   B: _____ (they)

   A: They're nice people.

5. *A:* I really liked my students last semester.

   B: Good. _____ (they)

   A: They loved to learn, and they loved to laugh.

   * scary: *frightening, making you afraid, e.g., a scary movie*

UNITS
48-49

What . . . ?, *Which . . . ?*, and *How . . . ?*
How long does it take . . . ?

Complete the questions. Read the answers first.

Questions

Answers

1. <u>What color</u>   is your car?   It's red.

2. <u>Which</u>   car is yours?   The blue one.

3. _____ does the   It opens at 10 A.M.
   library open?

4. _____ is the   It's 1,250 feet tall.
   Empire State Building?

5. _____ is your car?   There's room for four people.

6. _____ of fruit   I'd like an apple, please.
   would you like?

7. _____ is it to your office?   It's exactly 12 miles from here.

8. _____ is bigger,   Mexico City.
   Los Angeles or Mexico City?

9. _____ of job does   She's an accountant.
   Sally have?

10. _____ does it rain here?   It rains almost every day in the winter.

11. _____ was your TV?   It was around $300.

12. _____ would you   I'd like coffee, please.
    like, tea or coffee? I have both.

13. _____ is your brother?   He's six feet four inches tall.

14. _____ is older,   Paula.
    Paula or her husband?

15. _____ does it take   About nine hours.
    to drive to San Francisco?

What . . . ?, Which . . . ?, and *How . . . ?*
How long does it take . . . ?

Write questions with *What*, *Which*, *How*, etc. They should have the same meaning as the questions on the left.

1. Is your sister 12? 15?   *How old is your sister?*

2. Did you get up early? Late?   *What time did you get up?*

3. Is this sweater a large or a medium?   What _____ ?

4. Did you spend $20 on the present? $30?   _____

5. Do you like this shirt? Or that one?   _____

6. Have you been working here a long time? A short time?   _____

7. Do you like popular music? Classical? Jazz?   _____

8. Do you go to church every week? Once a month?   _____

9. Are her eyes brown? Green? Blue?   _____

10. Is the brown coat yours? The blue one?   _____

11. Does it take a year to learn a language? Two years?   _____

12. Were the flowers $10? $15?   _____

13. Will it take you an hour to drive to the beach? Two hours?   _____

14. Should we buy roses? Violets?   _____

15. Did it take you a week to paint your house? Two weeks?   _____

Do you know where . . . ?, I don't know what . . . , etc.

Write answers to the questions. Begin with any one of the following:
• I think I know . . . • I'm not sure . . . • I don't know . . . • No one knows . . .

1. Where is Ashgabad?

   I think I know where Ashgabad is.

2. Do fish have teeth?

   I don't know if fish have teeth.
   OR *I don't know whether fish have teeth.*

3. How many stars are there in the sky?

   No one knows how many stars there are in the sky.

4. What does "silly" mean?

5. Who was Abraham Lincoln?

6. How does a computer work?

7. Who did John F. Kennedy marry?

8. How many times have astronauts gone to the moon?

9. When was Mother Teresa born?

10. How long does it take to fly from Beijing to New York City?

11. How much does a house in Moscow cost?

12. How many calories are there in an apple?

13. Why do people make war?

14. How many people have died in wars?

15. Did it rain more a hundred years ago?

Questions

Write questions about a family. It can be about a real family or a family from a book. It can be a famous family or your own family.

1. Where _do the Westons usually go on vacation in summer_ ?

   Where _____ ?

2. What _did the Weston family do last summer_ ?

   What _____ ?

3. When _____ ?

4. Why _____ ?

5. Is _____ ?

6. Do _____ ?

7. Can someone tell me which _____ ?

8. Does anyone know what kind of _____ ?

9. Did _____ ?

10. Have _____ ?

11. _____ , does he?

12. _____ , didn't they?

13. How long does it take _____ ?

She said that . . . He told me that . . .

Reported Speech

Look at the pictures. They show what the people really did. Read what the people said. Complete the sentences about what they said and what they did. Use *said* or *told*.

1. Frank and Ashley said, "We'll be home early."

Frank and Ashley _said that they would be home early_ , but they got home very late.

2. Kate said, "I am a vegetarian*."

Kate _told_ me that _____

_____ , but the last time we were in a restaurant together she ordered chicken.

3. Larry said, "I am very sick today."

_____ that _____

_____ , but someone saw him at a baseball game.

4. Matt said, "I have to visit my aunt in the hospital."

_____ me that

_____ , but he went out dancing last night.

5. Alex and Susan said, "We are going to get up early on Saturday."

_____ that _____

_____ , but they slept late.

* vegetarian: *a person who doesn't eat meat*

EXERCISE CONTINUES ▶ ▶

6. Mrs. Holden said, "My son can play the violin beautifully."

_____ us that _____

_____ ,

but I don't think he can.

7. Bill's aunt said, "I have just sent you some money for your
birthday."

Last week _____ that

_____ , but he hasn't

received it.

8. Richard said, "I won't tell anyone your secret."

Richard _____ me

that _____ ,

but he told everyone.

9. Aunt Claudia said, "I don't eat sweets."

_____ that

_____ ,

but most of the chocolates are gone.

Work/working, go/going, do/doing

Complete the sentences so that they correctly describe the situation.

1. It rained this morning, so Leslie stayed home.

   Leslie stayed home because it was _raining_ this morning.

2. My parents are thinking of leaving town this weekend.

   My parents might _leave town this weekend_ .

3. My advice to you is, "Study harder."

   I think you should _____ .

4. I had trouble sleeping last night.

   I didn't _____ well _____ .

5. "I would love to go with you, but I have to watch my little brother now," Bob said.

   Bob can't _____ us because he is _____ right now.

6. *(on the phone)* Sorry, Adam isn't in right now. He's gone to lunch.

   Adam is _____ lunch outside the office.

7. It's late. I don't think your parents are awake anymore.

   It's late. Your parents must _____ asleep already.

8. Yesterday Jean said, "I need to do some shopping, but I don't have any money."

   Jean wanted _____, but she didn't _____ .

9. Judy called to talk to Gloria, but Gloria was in the bathtub.

   Judy couldn't _____ because Gloria was _____ a bath.

10. *Sid:* Does Ben still work for his brother?

    Nat: No, he got another job a few months ago.

    Ben used _____ , but he doesn't anymore.

11. *Lucy:* Do you want to go to lunch now?

    Clare: No, I need to wait for an important phone call.

    Clare isn't going to lunch now because she has _____ for a phone call.

To . . . (I want to do) and –ing (I enjoy doing)

Complete the sentences so that they correctly describe the situation. Use *to* . . . or *-ing*.

1. I asked Jeremy for help. He said, "No."

   Jeremy _____ refused _to help me_ _____ .

2. Do you like to stay home on weekends?

   Do you _____ enjoy _staying home on weekends_ _____ ?

3. My brother dreams of visiting Egypt one day.

   My brother would love _____ .

4. Could you give me a ride* to the doctor's tomorrow afternoon?

   Would you mind _____ ?

5. *Marlene:* Would you like me to give you a ride* home?

   You: No, thanks. I'd rather walk.

   Marlene offered _____ , but I preferred _____ .

6. *Elena:* Should we leave at seven tomorrow morning?

   Steve: How about 7:30? Seven is a little early.

   Elena suggested _____ , but Steve wanted _____ .

7. *Dan:* Let's go to the movies.

   Jean: Not right now. I want to finish writing my report for work.

   Dan wanted _____ , but Jean didn't want to

   stop _____ .

8. *Mother:* Why are you watching TV? Did you clean your room?

   Bev: Yes. I've cleaned it already.

   Bev has finished _____ .

9. How about going to the mountains this weekend?

   Would you like _____ ?

10. "A lawyer has a very boring job. I would rather be a teacher," Jim said.

    Jim would hate _____ a lawyer. He'd prefer _____ .

    * give someone a ride: *to take someone somewhere in a car*

To . . . (I want to do) and *-ing (I enjoy doing)*
I want you to . . . and *I told you to . . .*

Read the conversation. Then complete the description of the conversation. Use *to . . .* or *-ing*.

1. *Sylvia:* Use your credit card to pay for the tickets. It's faster.

   Nathan: You're right, but I think I'll pay by check.

   She told *him to use his credit card to pay for the tickets* . He decided
   to pay by check .

2. *Mother:* Can't you pick up your dirty clothes?

   Son: I guess I can, but I don't want to.

   The mother wanted _____ , but he refused
   _____ them up.

3. *Martin:* Let's go to the beach on Saturday.

   Wanda: OK, I like to be out in the sun on weekends.

   He suggested _____ . She said she enjoyed
   _____ .

4. *Jonathan:* I don't know why you don't want to buy this jacket. It looks nice on you.

   Jennie: I think it's too expensive, but I'll buy it if you think I should.

   Jonathan persuaded _____ the jacket, which
   she didn't want _____ at first.

5. *Jason:* Officer, can I leave now?

   Police officer: No, you'll have to wait.

   The police officer made _____ .

6. *Boss:* Can you work on Saturday?

   Bert: That's fine. I don't have anything else to do.

   The boss asked _____ , and Bert didn't mind
   _____ that day.

UNIT
55

I went to the store to . . .

Complete the sentences, keeping the same meaning. Use *to* and *for* where necessary.

1. I'm not going to Miami for Christmas. It costs too much.

    I don't have enough money *to go to Miami for Christmas*   .

2. I'm standing here because I need to ask the teacher about the test.

    I'm waiting to _____ .

3. Nicole flew to Quebec to go to a wedding.

    Nicole flew to Quebec for _____ .

4. I went to Ellen's party because I wanted to relax and meet new people.

    I went to Ellen's party to _____ .

5. Can you help me with my Arabic? Or are you too busy?

    Do you have enough time _____ .

6. I can't leave yet. The babysitter* hasn't come yet.

    I'm waiting _____ come.

7. Ron borrowed $20 from me for a present.

    Ron borrowed $20 from me to _____ .

8. When I finish this book, I'm going to give it to Wally. He's waiting.

    Wally is waiting for _____ the book.

9. Sophie is taking a class. She is learning how to use a computer.

    Sophie is taking a class to _____ .

10. Mrs. Nickels went to Brazil. She went to a conference there.

    Mrs. Nickels went to Brazil for _____ .

11. Answer my question. I'm waiting.

    I'm waiting for _____ my question.

   * babysitter: *person who takes care of children in their home when the parents are out*

Use your own ideas to complete the sentences. Begin your answer with a verb in the base form (*work/go*), *to . . . (to work / to go)*, or *-ing (working/going)*.

1. When visitors come to my town, I usually suggest <u>*visiting the museum downtown*</u> .
   When visitors come to my town, I usually suggest <u>*going to the mountains near the city*</u> .
   When visitors come to my town, I usually suggest <u>*staying in one of our nice, old hotels*</u> .
   When visitors come to my town, I usually suggest _____ .

2. A lot of people want _____ .

3. When I was little, I used _____ .

4. I can't _____ because _____ .

5. My friends and I couldn't _____ because we didn't _____ .

6. I usually enjoy _____ .

7. When I am busy, I sometimes forget _____ .

8. If you want _____ well, you need _____ .

9. I hate _____ , but I don't mind _____ .

10. The father often told his children, "I want you _____
    _____ , but I don't want you _____ ."

11. I wanted _____ , but I couldn't persuade _____ .

12. Sometimes people ask me _____ .

13. I am learning English _____ .

14. I refused _____ because _____ .

15. Sometimes I think I should _____ because I don't _____ .

16. I would like _____ , but it might _____ .

REVIEW
-ing and *to*

**Use your own ideas to complete the sentences. Add a verb in the base form
(*work/go*), to . . . (*to work / to go*), or *-ing* (*working/going*).**

1. I don't mind *traveling alone* , but I really prefer *to travel with other people*
   OR *traveling with other people*   .
   I don't mind _____ , but I really prefer _____ .

2. I was _____ when someone started _____ .

3. I used _____ , but I don't _____ anymore.

4. I can't _____ because I am _____ .

5. I love _____ , but I don't enjoy _____ .

6. They didn't let _____ because they expected _____ .

7. My doctor often advises _____ , but I sometimes
   forget _____ .

8. I couldn't persuade _____ , so I tried _____ .

9. My teacher suggested _____ , but I couldn't _____ .

10. I didn't _____ , and I don't _____ .

11. I was planning _____ , but I decided _____ .

12. I should _____ , but I will probably _____ instead.

13. I can _____ , but I would hate _____ .

14. My boss asked _____ , but he didn't make _____ .

15. I went _____ for _____ .

EXERCISE 68

Go to ... go on ... go for ... go -ing

Use *go* in an appropriate form and the correct word(s) from the box to complete the sentences. Use *to*, *on*, or *for* if necessary.

a business trip	a movie	drugstore / some aspirin	strike*	shopping	skiing
Poland / vacation	swimming	the supermarket	a walk	work	

1. It's hot. Why don't we _go swimming_ ?

2. *(on the phone)* I can't talk to you now. I have to _go to the supermarket_ to buy some rice and other things for dinner.

3. The Thompsons _____ last week. They are visiting relatives there.

4. We _____ in Colorado next winter if there's enough snow.

5. We need some exercise. Let's _____ before dinner.

6. Mrs. Lopez travels a lot in her job. In fact, she's _____ to New York later this week.

7. *A:* Where's Ariana?

   B: She has _____ for some birthday presents. She'll be back soon.

8. What time are you _____ tomorrow? I need a ride to the library next to your office.

9. I'd like to go out with you tonight, but I'm _____ with a friend. You can join us if you want.

10. I'm _____ . Do we need anything else?

11. That shoe factory isn't producing anything. The workers _____ last week.

   * strike: *refusal to work*

EXERCISE 69

Get

Complete the sentences with the correct form of *get* and the words in parentheses. Sometimes you need to add *in*, *on*, *off*, *out of*, or *to*.

1. *A:* Are you ready to leave yet?

   B: No, I still have to _get dressed_ _____ (dressed).

2. *A:* Is that young couple married?

   B: Yes. They _____ (married) last year.

3. I'm _____ (tired). I think I'll go to bed.

4. I couldn't find a seat when I _____ (the bus) this morning.
   But I found a seat when some people _____ (the bus)
   at the museum.

5. Poor Diane. She forgot her briefcase when she _____ (the taxi)
   this morning.

6. Can I stand under your umbrella? I'm _____ (wet).

7. *A:* *(in an office)* Hello, I'm here to see Mrs. Rossi.

   B: One minute, please. I'll _____ (her) for you.

8. *A:* What time shall I call you?

   B: I usually _____ (home) about 5:30, so any time after that.

9. *A:* Sorry I didn't _____ (here) earlier to help out. I took
   the wrong turn and _____ (lost).

   B: That's all right. We are still _____ (ready) for the
   party. You can help us with some last-minute things.

10. *A:* We're going skiing in the mountains this weekend.

    B: How nice. How long does it take to _____ (there)?

    A: About three hours.

11. My boss will be angry if I _____ (work) late again.

12. Five people _____ (the car) before Reggie, so there was
    no room for him.

Complete the paragraphs with the correct form of *do* or *make*.

Last week I **1)** _made_ a stupid mistake. While I was **2)** _____ the dishes one morning, my tooth started to hurt. It was too early to call the dentist, so I asked my brother, "Can you **3)** _____ me a favor?"

"Sure, what is it?" he asked.

"Could you **4)** _____ a phone call for me later? I need to **5)** _____ an appointment with Dr. Greer, but I have a lot to **6)** _____ at the office this morning, and I won't have time to call," I said.

"I'll **7)** _____ my best to get you an appointment. What day do you want it for?" he asked.

"Tomorrow is OK, but if he can see me this afternoon, so much the better," I answered. I **8)** _____ a little more housework and then left for work. But my toothache was getting worse.

I called my brother from work at lunchtime. "What are you **9)** _____ ?" I asked.

"I just finished **10)** _____ my laundry, and now I'm **11)** _____ myself lunch. I called Dr. Greer, and he can see you at 4 P.M. today," my brother said.

"I'm lucky he can see me today," I said. "Thanks for **12)** _____ this for me. I'll see you after my appointment."

When I got to my dentist's office, I realized what I had **13)** _____ . My dentist's name is Dr. Philips. I had asked my brother to call Dr. Greer, my regular doctor, not my dentist. I still had a toothache, and Dr. Philips's office was closed for the day. "What should I **14)** _____ now?" I thought to myself. In the end, I just went home, took two aspirins, asked my brother not to **15)** _____ too much noise, and went to bed.

Luckily, my toothache was gone the next morning. I didn't have to see the dentist this time, but I know that I'll have to **16)** _____ something about my tooth soon.

Have

What do you say in these situations? Use *have* or *have got* in the correct form and the words in parentheses.

1. Your friend had a party for her mother's birthday. Ask your friend where it was.

   (you / the party) *Where did you have the party?*

2. Your sister is holding her head and looks sick. What do you ask her?

   (a headache) *Do you have a headache?* OR *Have you got a headache?*

3. Andrew lost his driver's license. He had a lot of accidents. Ask him about the accidents.

   (How many) _____

4. You arrive home late with your brother. You can't find your key. Ask your brother about his key.

   (your key) _____

5. Eric looks a little nervous when he gets off the plane. Ask about his flight.

   (bad) _____

6. Your friend's sister was expecting a baby the last time you saw her. Ask about the baby.

   (your sister / her baby / yet) _____

7. Your friend Sarah hasn't talked to her brother for six months. Perhaps there was an argument.* Ask her.

   (you / with) _____

8. Mike missed work last week. Many other people were out with the flu. Ask Mike if that was his problem.

   (last week) _____

9. Your friends just came home from a concert. What do you ask them?

   (a good time / at the concert) _____

   * argument: *a fight, a disagreement*

Complete the conversations with the correct form of *do*, *get*, *have*, or *make*.

1. *A:* Who _does_ _____ the cooking at your house?

   B: My dad. My mom _gets_ _____ home from work too late to cook.

2. *A:* Does your husband _____ housework?

   B: Not often. He _____ dinner on the weekends, but I

   have to _____ all the cleaning.

   A: But you _____ a job now. That doesn't seem fair.

   B: It isn't. But his mother _____ everything for him when he was young. He has

   been that way since we _____ married.

3. *A:* Who's _____ all that noise?

   B: The students next door must be _____ a party again.

   Stay calm – don't _____ angry.

   A: It's hard to _____ my homework with that loud music playing. I know

   I'll _____ a lot of mistakes because I just can't concentrate* with all
   the noise.

   B: I'll _____ dressed and go next door to ask them to be quiet.

4. *A:* *(on a bus)* Let's _____ off the bus at the next stop. I'm _____
   tired of standing – I'd rather walk.

   B: Look, you can _____ that seat. There's a free one over there now. I'll stand.

5. *A:* Tomorrow morning, can you remind me to _____ a phone call?

   B: Sure. Who do you need to call?

   A: The dentist. I need to _____ an appointment for a cleaning.

6. *A:* Did you _____ a good time in Florida?

   B: Yes, it was wonderful. We _____ breakfast by the ocean every

   morning. We didn't have to _____ laundry or the dishes.

   In fact, we didn't _____ any work all week. We didn't even have to

   _____ our beds.

   A: Lucky you!

   * concentrate: *to keep your attention on something*

UNITS
56-59

Go, get, do, make, and have

Use your own ideas to write sentences with the words in parentheses.

1. (do housework / never) _We never do housework on Saturday._
   OR _I never did housework before, but I have to do it now._
   _____

2. (go to bed / late) _____
   _____

3. (get to work / early) _____
   _____

4. (get married / soon) _____
   _____

5. (have a baby / not long ago) _____
   _____

6. (go shopping / at lunchtime) _____
   _____

7. (have an accident / a while ago) _____
   _____

8. (make / a terrible mistake) _____
   _____

9. (have a party / on my birthday) _____
   _____

10. (get ready / after) _____
    _____

11. (do exercises / at night) _____
    _____

12. (make a list / before) _____
    _____

UNIT 60

I/me, he/him, they/them, etc.

Complete the conversations. Use an appropriate form of like (like/likes, don't/doesn't like, or do/does . . . like). Use the correct form of pronouns (I/me, you, she/her, etc.).

A's Statement or Question	**B's Response**
1. Why doesn't Laurie eat spaghetti?	*She doesn't like it.*
2. I met my fiancé's parents last night.	Really? *Do you like them?*
3. Eric is really nice, and so is his sister.	I agree. _____ both a lot.
4. Are those your new shoes?	Yes. _____ ?
5. My sons are taking swimming lessons at the park.	Really? _____ ?
6. Samantha, you never eat food from the cafeteria. Why not?	Well, _____ very much.
7. Why does Jim's dog bark every time we visit?	Maybe _____ .
8. Does your brother want to go to college in the west or in the east?	The west. _____ better.
9. Why does Liz want to sell her sofa?	_____ anymore. She wants to buy a new one.
10. I always invite Ahmed and his family when we have a party.	It seems that you _____ a lot.
11. Would your father like cream in his coffee?	Yes. _____ black.
12. Is Sarah going to buy that expensive jacket?	No. _____ , but she doesn't have enough money to buy it.
13. So, why don't you eat tomatoes?	_____ , but I can't eat them. They make me feel sick.
14. Are the Simons going to eat at their usual restaurant?	No. _____ anymore. They say the prices have gone up a lot, and the food isn't as good as it was.

I/me, he/him, they/them, etc.

Complete the questions with *I, me, he, him,* etc.

1. Carol wants to borrow Bob's car. Will he lend *it* to *her* ?

2. I'd like to meet Mrs. Chang. Would you introduce *her* to *me* ?

3. The Kennedys want to see your house. Will you show _____ to _____ ?

4. I'd like to borrow your car. Will you lend _____ to _____ ?

5. My parents want to go to a concert Saturday night. Can you take _____ to _____ ?

6. We don't understand pages 22 to 24. Will the teacher explain _____ to _____ ?

7. I didn't see the accident. Could you describe _____ to _____ ?

8. The police didn't see the woman who left the scene of the accident*. Can you describe _____ to _____ ?

9. You want to look at my newspaper? I can lend _____ to _____ for a few minutes.

10. My mother would like to see the flowers in George's garden. Do you think he will show _____ to _____ ?

11. They didn't hear the joke. Can you tell _____ to _____ ?

12. I left my papers in your office. Would you bring _____ to _____ ?

13. Dad left his lunch at home. Can you take _____ to _____ ?

14. I'd like some butter, please. Can you pass _____ to _____ ?

15. Sally would like some more beans. Could you pass _____ to _____ ?

16. I didn't get Mr. Ricci's e-mail. Can you send _____ to _____ ?

17. Richard didn't understand the directions. Can you explain _____ to _____ again?

18. Miranda doesn't know our friends. Can you introduce _____ to _____ ?

* scene of the accident: *place where the accident happened*

My/his/their, etc.
Whose is this? It's mine/yours/theirs, etc.
I, me, my, and *mine*

Read the situation. Check (✔) the best description.

1. We took their luggage to his hotel room.

   _✔_ a. My parents had a suitcase. We left it in my brother's room at the hotel.

   _____ b. My sister had a lot of luggage, so we helped her to the room with it.

   _____ c. My two brothers each had a suitcase. We needed room in the car, so we put the suitcases in my sister's room.

2. She used your towel. Why don't you use hers?

   _____ a. You can use Sarah's towel because she used yours by mistake.

   _____ b. Don't use Sarah's towel. There's another one that John hasn't used yet.

   _____ c. I'll give you and Sarah clean towels.

3. Ours is broken, so she used theirs.

   _____ a. Our lawn mower* isn't working. Anna borrowed her son's lawn mower.

   _____ b. Anna didn't have a lawn mower, so she borrowed one from us.

   _____ c. Anna borrowed our neighbors' lawn mower because our lawn mower needs to be repaired.

4. Yours is difficult, but I think hers is more difficult.

   _____ a. Your job is easier than Jane's.

   _____ b. I think you worker harder than Jane.

   _____ c. Ted and Jane have harder jobs than you do.

5. Mine are blue, but his are brown.

   _____ a. I have a blue suitcase, but my brother has a brown one.

   _____ b. Joe has brown suitcases. I have blue suitcases.

   _____ c. Sarah's suitcases are brown, but my suitcases are blue.

6. *A:* Is this his or hers?
   B: Neither. It's ours.

   _____ a. The keys don't belong to John or Maria; they belong to us.

   _____ b. This key belongs to John and Maria.

   _____ c. This key belongs to us, not to John or Maria.

   * lawn mower: *a machine used for cutting grass*

NITS
1-63,
97

My/his/their, etc.
Whose is this? It's mine/yours/theirs, etc.
I, me, my, and *mine*

Read the paragraphs. Then complete them with *I, me, my, mine*, etc.

Barbara, a co-worker, can be a difficult person. Recently, I lent Barbara 1) _my_
pen at work because she didn't have 2) _hers_ that day. But 3) _it_
was a present from a friend, so I wanted 4) _____ back. I asked 5) _____
to return 6) _____ as soon as possible. Yesterday she told 7) _____
that she had lost the pen. She's so careless!

I am not the only person who has a problem with Barbara. Just last week Ben gave
8) _____ extra pair of reading glasses to 9) _____ because she had
left 10) _____ at home. She promised 11) _____ that she would
return 12) _____ the next day, but Ben still doesn't have his glasses.

One time, Barbara asked two co-workers for part of 13) _____ lunch.
"I forgot 14) _____ on the train," she explained. They generously gave her
some of 15) _____ . Then she borrowed a dollar from 16) _____
to get something to drink! They weren't very happy.

Yesterday was the worst! She came into 17) _____ office and took my chair.
When I asked her what she was doing, she said, "I didn't know it was 18) _____ .
I thought it was 19) _____." She's impossible.

Myself/yourself/themselves, etc.

Look at the picture. Rewrite the sentences to correct them. Use pronouns ending with *–self* or *–selves* or *each other* where possible.

AT THE PARK

1. A young woman is sitting by herself.

   A young man is sitting by himself.

2. Two women are sitting on the same bench and talking to themselves.

   _____

3. The girls on the swings are enjoying themselves.

   _____

4. The young man and young woman on rollerblades are waving at themselves.

   _____

EXERCISE CONTINUES ▶ ▶

5. The child is saying, "I want to feed the pigeons by herself."

_____

6. A girl with a dog is angry at herself. The dog is enjoying itself, however.

_____

7. The boy with the skateboard hurt someone when he fell.

_____

8. The woman is telling her two friends, "Enjoy yourself at the park."

_____

–'s (Kate's camera / my brother's car, etc.)

Use a word or phrase from the box and the words in parentheses to complete each sentence.

the bottom	the color	the condition	doctor
~~husband~~	in-laws*	job	little girl and boy
names	party	~~roof~~	wives

1. _My aunt's husband_ _____ (my aunt) is a nice man.

2. _The roof of this building_ _____ (this building) needs repair.

3. _____ (my father) isn't interesting, but the salary is good.

4. We had fun at _____ (Susan), but she didn't enjoy herself much because she was busy with serving food.

5. _____ (my uncles) are lawyers.

6. _____ (your package) is wet. Is there a bottle inside?

7. Do you see _____ (brother) very often, or do he and his family live far away?

8. I didn't recognize you! You changed _____ (your hair).

9. Mikey and Annie are really _____ (children). We would usually call adults Mike and Ann.

10. _____ (my son) are coming to dinner. I've never met them before.

11. My dentist said, " _____ (your teeth) is terrible."

12. _____ (Kathy) told her she was in perfect health.

* in-laws: *your husband's or wife's relatives, such as his or her parents*

EXERCISE 80

Pronouns and Possessives

Use your own ideas to write sentences with the words in parentheses.

1. (his / my / mine) _My brother likes his English teacher, but I think mine is better._
   OR _My friend lost her calculator, so she borrowed mine._
   _____
   _____

2. (my friend's / him) _____

3. (the beginning / the story) _____

4. (my parents' / them) _____

5. (ourselves / hurt) _____

6. (themselves / him) _____

7. (by yourselves / with each other) _____

8. (each other / angry) _____

9. (hers / my) _____

10. (theirs / mine) _____

11. (think / himself) _____

12. (the telephone number / that company) _____

13. (they / us / it) _____

UNITS
66-67

A/an . . .
Flower(s) and ***bus(es)*** (Singular and Plural)

A and The

The information in the sentences doesn't match the picture. Correct the sentences. Use the appropriate form (singular or plural) of the nouns and verbs in the sentences. Use *a/an* correctly.

1. There's a mirror on the wall of the restaurant.

   There are two mirrors on the wall of the restaurant.

2. There are two families in the restaurant.

   There is a family in the restaurant.

3. This is a Chinese restaurant.

   _____

4. There's a child in the family.

   _____

5. The mother is wearing shorts.

   _____

6. The boy is wearing long pants and a shirt.

   _____

7. There is a flower on each table.

   _____

EXERCISE CONTINUES ▶ ▶

8. There's a shelf on the back wall of the restaurant.

_____

9. There's a dish on the top shelf.

_____

10. There are a knife, a fork, and a spoon on the middle shelf.

_____

11. There's a bowl with some apples on the bottom shelf.

_____

12. There are some mice under one of the tables.

_____

13. The restaurant is open for an hour at lunchtime.

_____

14. Two women are ordering food.

_____

15. There's a fish in the fish tank.

_____

A/an . . .
Flower(s) and *bus(es)* (Singular and Plural)
A car, some money (Countable and Uncountable)

Complete the sentences with the words in parentheses and *a/an* or *–s* if necessary.

1. (oil, stove, tea, teapot, tomato, water)
   a. To make tea, you need *a stove, tea, a teapot, and water* .
   b. You don't need *oil or tomatoes* OR *oil or a tomato* .

2. (computer, glue, place to work, ruler, tool, university class, wood)

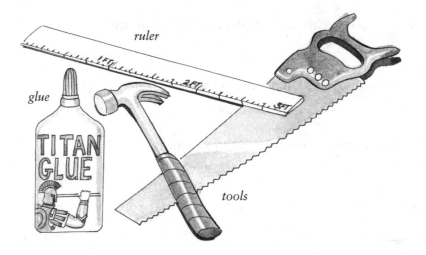

glue
ruler
tools

   a. To make a chair, you need _____
      _____ .
   b. You don't need _____
      _____ .

3. (dentist, guitar, long hair, lesson, person to listen, orchestra, piano, piece of music, teacher, test, time to practice)
   a. To learn to play the guitar, it is helpful to have _____
      _____ .
   b. You don't need _____
      _____ .

EXERCISE CONTINUES ▶ ▶

4. (blanket, car, carpet, diamond, dish, fork, furniture, money, pillow, pot and pan, refrigerator, stove, towel, vegetable)

   a. To furnish an apartment, a couple needs _____

   _____ .

   b. They don't need _____

   _____ .

5. (engineer, garden, hammer, knife, scissors, seed, shovel, soil, water)

shovel

   a. To grow flowers, you need _____

   _____ .

   b. You don't need _____

   _____ .

6. (dictionary, idea, information, new hat, paper, time to think, TV program)

   a. To write an essay, a student needs _____

   _____ .

   b. A student doesn't need _____

   _____ .

A car, some money (Countable and Uncountable)

Complete the sentences with the nouns in parentheses and *a/an* or *–s* where necessary. Use *some* where possible.

1. (music, walk)

   A: To relax, I sometimes take *a walk* .

   B: Really? I just listen to *some music* when I'm nervous.

2. (piece of chicken, rice)

   A: What did you have for dinner?

   B: Just _____ and _____ .

3. (bread, can of beans)

   A: What did you buy at the store?

   B: _____ and two _____ .

4. (long brown hair, small nose, eye)

   A: How will I know your daughter when I see her?

   B: She has _____ , _____ and blue _____ .

5. (new suitcase, warm clothing)

   A: What do we need for our trip?

   B: We need _____ and two _____ .

6. (bottle of perfume, earring)

   A: What would Gloria like for her birthday?

   B: I'm not sure. I bought her _____ and _____ .

7. (ice cream, apple)

   A: *(at the supermarket)* Should we buy _____ ? They look good.

   B: No, I'd rather get _____ .

8. (glass of water, lemonade)

   A: I've drunk three _____ and I'm still thirsty.

   B: Why don't you have _____ ?

A/an and the
Go to work   go home   go to the movies
I like music. I hate exams.

Read the story. Write *a, an,* or *the* in each blank. If nothing is needed in a blank, write *X*.

Many families have trouble finding time to spend together. Parents often get **1)** $\underline{\quad X \quad}$ home from **2)** _____ work late, and children often have many after-school activities, such as music or swimming lessons. It is difficult for them to have **3)** _____ dinner together as **4)** _____ family. The Khan family is an example.

Until recently, the Khan family didn't eat together often. Mr. and Mrs. Khan and their two children – Michael and Sara – were all busy. **5)** _____ parents were busy with their schedules at **6)** _____ work, and **7)** _____ children were busy with their schedules at **8)** _____ school and after **9)** _____ school. The members of **10)** _____ family ate something from **11)** _____ refrigerator or they warmed something in **12)** _____ microwave. Often they ate **13)** _____ fast food*. They used to eat at different times, and they usually didn't have their meals in **14)** _____ dining room. Sometimes family members ate in **15)** _____ living room in front of **16)** _____ television. As a result, they weren't having very healthy meals.

Now the family has tried to change its habits. The family members eat two meals together: The parents fix **17)** _____ simple breakfast and **18)** _____ big hot meal in the evening. For **19)** _____ dinner, they usually have **20)** _____ chicken or fish with **21)** _____ rice or **22)** _____ potatoes. They sometimes have **23)** _____ pasta. They always have **24)** _____ big salad. And they often have **25)** _____ fruit for dessert. Sometimes they get **26)** _____ take-out food from **27)** _____ restaurant to eat at **28)** _____ home. After they eat, the four of them often watch **29)** _____ TV or **30)** _____ video together. Sometimes, they go to **31)** _____ movies, but not on weeknights.

Everyone in **32)** _____ family is happier with the decision to spend more time together and to eat **33)** _____ better meals.

   * fast food: *food that can be cooked easily or that can be sold quickly in restaurants, like hamburgers, etc.*

The . . . (Names of Places)

Answer the questions about the words in parentheses, adding *the* where necessary. If you are not sure of the answer, begin with *I think* . . . .

1. Which has more water? (Mississippi River, Indian Ocean)

   The Indian Ocean has more water than the Mississippi River.

2. Which is bigger? (London Zoo, Grand Canyon National Park)

3. Where are there more people? (Indonesia, United Arab Emirates)

4. Which has more old things? (Museum of Science and Industry in Chicago, Vatican Museums)

5. Which mountains are higher? (Himalayas, Alps)

6. Which has a larger population? (Western Europe, Asia)

7. Which country has more land? (Philippines, Japan)

8. Which is taller? (Washington Monument, Empire State Building)

9. Which is older? (Colosseum, Great Wall of China)

10. Which street in New York is more famous? (Wall Street, Columbus Avenue)

11. In the Northern Hemisphere, where do more cold winds come from? (north, south)

Use your own ideas to write sentences with the words in parentheses. Use the phrases as they are given, with or without *a/an* – do not change them. The verbs can be in any appropriate form.

1. (last month / next week) *I went to the doctor's last month, but I have to go again next week. OR I hope it will be warmer next week because it has been cold here since last month.*

2. (the radio / TV) _____

3. (an apple / the orange) _____

4. (an engineer / an hour) _____

5. (a salad / some pizza) _____

6. (a book / the floor / the book) _____

7. (the hotel / a car) _____

8. (go to work / return home) _____

9. (friends / the friends) _____

10. (information / the newspaper) _____

11. (a letter / advice) _____

This/these and *that/those*

Determiners and Pronouns

A. Match B's responses to A's statements and questions.

A

_c_ 1. Are these your gloves?

____ 2. *(on the phone)* Hello. Is this Tom?

____ 3. The problem is your fault.

____ 4. Is this Mr. North's coat?

____ 5. Excuse me, is this seat taken?

____ 6. Which flowers do you like better?

____ 7. Which watermelon should we buy?

____ 8. Mark got very angry at me yesterday.

____ 9. Cindy, this is my brother, Jim.

____ 10. Who is that man?

B

a. This one looks better than that one.

b. Nice to meet you.

✔ c. No, they aren't. I don't have any.

d. I think these look a little fresher than those.

e. That's unfair. It's not true.

f. I think it's Amy's dad.

g. No, it isn't. He's not at work today.

h. No, it's mine.

i. That's too bad. I'm sorry to hear it.

j. Yes, but there's a free one over there.

B. Complete the teacher's questions and the students' answers. Use the words in parentheses.

Teacher's questions	Students' answers
1. (cap) *Is this your cap?*	Yes, *it is.*
2. (keys) *Are these your keys?*	No, *they aren't.*

EXERCISE CONTINUES ▶ ▶

3. (pencils) _____   Yes, _____ .
   _____

4. (lunch) _____   No, _____ .
   _____

5. (book) _____   No, _____ .
   _____

6. (pictures) _____   Yes, _____ .
   _____

Teacher's questions	**Students' answers**

7. (glasses) *Are those your glasses?*   Yes, they _____ .

8. (backpack) *Is that your backpack?*   No, it _____ .

9. (scissors) _____   Yes, _____ .
   _____

10. (apple) _____   Yes, _____ .
    _____

11. (bottle of water) _____   No, _____ .
    _____

12. (soccer shoes) _____   No, _____ .
    _____

One/ones
Some and *any*

Complete the conversations with *some*, *any*, or *one/ones* and the words in parentheses. Add any other necessary words. Put the verbs in the correct form.

1. *A:* Are you going to lend money to Jake?
   B: (not / have) No, *I don't have any* .

2. *A:* Would you like to see a movie tonight?
   B: (there / be / good) Yes, if *there is a good one* in town.

3. *A:* Should I buy flowers at the store?
   B: (look for / nice, fresh) Yes. _____

4. *A:* Should I get coffee at the store?
   B: (not / need) No, we _____ .

5. *A:* Are these gloves too big?
   B: Yes. (you / have / smaller?) _____

6. *A:* What kinds of restaurants does Paul like?
   B: (eat / in expensive) He only _____ .

7. *A:* We stayed at a nice hotel in Chicago.
   B: (you / stay) Which _____ at?
   A: A hotel downtown – I forget the name.

8. *A:* (we / need / rice?) _____
   B: (have) No, we _____ .

9. *A:* What kind of car are you looking for?
   B: (look for / small / with four doors) We _____
   _____ .

10. *A:* Why is Julia so lonely here?
    B: (not / have / friends) She _____ .

NITS
8-79

Not + any, no, and none
Not + anybody/anyone/anything, and nobody, no one, and nothing

A. Rewrite the sentences with *no*.

1. I don't have any time to waste. *I have no time to waste.*

2. There aren't any new people on the list. _____

3. This store doesn't have any fresh tomatoes. _____

4. There isn't any reason for you to stay home tonight. _____

5. Mr. Ryan doesn't have any patience with his children. _____

6. I didn't have any problems with your car. _____

7. There isn't any milk in the refrigerator. _____

8. There aren't any clouds in the sky today. _____

B. Answer the questions two ways in the negative: (1) with a short answer, and (2) with a complete sentence.

1. Who are you talking to?
   No one.   *I'm not talking to anyone.*

2. What did you buy?
   Nothing.   *I didn't buy anything.*

3. How many cars are there in the driveway?
   None.   *There aren't any cars in the driveway.*

4. What did they say about me?
   _____   _____

5. What are you angry about?
   _____   _____

6. Who are you angry at?
   _____   _____

7. How much money did you spend?
   _____   _____

8. What are you listening to?
   _____   _____

UNIT
80

Somebody, anything, nowhere, etc.

Complete the conversations with *somebody, anything, nowhere,* etc.

1. *Doctor:* Is there _anything_____ wrong with your hearing?

   Patient: No, _nothing_____ at all. Why do you ask?

   Doctor: I just thought there might be _____ wrong because you complained of an earache the last time you were here.

2. *A:* I think there is _____ at the door. Can you check?

   B: (after a minute) No, there is _____ . But I think _____ rang the bell next door.

3. *A:* The boss said _____ surprising to me the other day.

   B: Really? Did he say _____ about raises*?

   A: No, it didn't have _____ to do with money. It was about working on the weekend.

   B: You're kidding*! _____ is going to come in to work on the weekend. Doesn't he know that?

4. *A:* Do you live _____ near Tom?

   B: No. Why?

   A: He left _____ at my house yesterday, and I want to return it to him.

   B: It is not very easy for me, but I'll take it to him if you want me to.

5. *A:* Did Roger give you _____ for your birthday?

   B: No. Actually, he never gives _____ to _____ .

6. *A:* Helen said she wasn't going to go _____ for vacation. In the end, she did go _____ .

   B: Really? Where?

   A: To Hawaii. She knows _____ there, so she didn't have to pay _____ for a place to stay.

   B: Good for her.

* raise: *an increase in salary*
* you're kidding: *you're not serious*

Every and *all*
All, most, some, any, and *no/none*

Write a sentence with the same meaning as the one given. Use the words in parentheses.

1. All plants need water.
   (every) *Every plant needs water.*

2. No one can live without food.
   (all / people / need) _____

3. There are no fresh flowers for sale today.
   (not any) _____

4. None of the secretaries were late this morning.
   (all / on time) _____

5. Some people like to live in the city.
   (some / not / in the country) _____

6. All of my friends have driver's licenses except one or two.
   (most) _____

7. Not all the students in my class study hard.
   (not every) _____

8. All of my cousins live in other states.
   (none / in this state) _____

9. All drivers have to have insurance in this state.
   (every) _____

10. All the people in my office are married.
    (everybody) _____

Every and *all*
All, most, some, any, and *no/none*

Look at the pictures from a picnic. The first shows the beginning of the picnic, and the second shows the end. Answer the questions. Use *all, most, some,* or *none + of them / of it.*

BEFORE   AFTER

1. How many of the apples were eaten? _Some of them were eaten._

2. How much of the bread is left? _None of it is left._

3. How much of the chicken is left? _____

4. How much of the salad was eaten? _____

5. How many of the sodas were drunk? _____

6. How much of the iced tea was drunk? _____

7. How much of the watermelon was eaten? _____

8. How many of the plates were used? _____

9. How much of the cake was eaten? _____

All, most, some, any, and no/none
Both, either, and neither

Look at the information about the four Smith children. Then answer the questions. Use *all, most, none, both, either,* or *neither + of*.

The Smith children	Paul	Sam	Hannah	Amy
Age?	29	23	24	20
Married?	yes	yes	engaged	no
Children?	3	1	no	no
Job?	engineer	salesperson	unemployed computer engineer	student
In school?	no	yes, at night	part-time	yes
Cook?	yes	yes	yes	yes
Exercise?	no	no	yes	yes
City	Chicago (in his own home)	Chicago (in his own apartment)	Chicago (in her own apartment)	Chicago (in a school dormitory*)

1. How many of the Smith children are over 30? *None of them are over 30.*

2. Are the boys married? Yes, both _____ .

3. Are the girls married? No, _____ .

4. Do the boys have children? Yes, _____ .

5. How many of them live in Chicago? _____

6. Do any of them live with the parents? No, _____ .

7. Which brother does Amy live with? _____

8. Do all of them have jobs? No. _____ the boys
_____ , but _____ the girls does.

9. Which of the children is a lawyer? _____

10. Which sister is a teacher? _____

11. Are any of them in school? Yes, _____ .

12. Do any of them know how to cook? Yes, _____ .

13. Do they exercise? _____ exercise, but _____
_____ does.

* dormitory: *a building at a school where students live*

UNITS
84-85
A lot of, much, and *many*
A little / a few and *little/few*

A. Write sentences that make sense with* the first sentence. Use the words in parentheses and *much, many,* or *a lot (of).* Use verbs in the present.

1. Jason doesn't read very much. (not / have / books) *He doesn't have many books*
   OR . . . *a lot of books.*

2. Sue is very thin. (not / eat) *She doesn't eat much.* OR *She doesn't eat a lot.*

3. Tina loves movies. (go / to the movies) _____

4. Ahmed is a good father. (give / love / to his children) _____

5. Alice is very busy. (not / have / free time) _____

6. Bill's life is hard. (have / problems) _____

7. They eat out a lot. (not / eat / at home) _____

8. Jerry is very pleasant and funny. (have / friends) _____

B. Complete the sentences. Use *very little, very few, a little,* or *a few.*

1. My car is very reliable. I have *very few* _____ problems with it.

2. *A:* Does your tooth hurt?
   B: Yes, it hurts *a little.* _____ .

3. Carlos watches TV almost every night. He goes out _____ .

4. *A:* Do you like your new computer?
   B: Yes, but sometimes I have _____ trouble with it.

5. *A:* Did you buy anything at the store?
   B: Yes, I bought _____ things.

6. The bus was almost empty. There were _____ people on it this morning.

7. Emily looks almost the same as she did ten years ago. She has changed _____ in the last ten years.

8. Tom's Japanese is almost perfect. He makes _____ mistakes.

* make sense with: *to go together logically; to be reasonable together*

A lot of, much, and *many*
A little / a few and *little/few*

Read the story. Circle the best answer.

Ray's car is getting old. It is always breaking down*. **1)** (A few) / A little / Few days ago, his car broke down* again. He has spent **2)** a lot of / many / much money fixing the car in the past, and he doesn't want to spend very **3)** a lot / many / much on it anymore. He has very **4)** a little / few / little money right now, so he can't buy another car. So he decided to fix the car himself. After all, there are **5)** a lot / many / much people who fix their own cars to save money. These days there are very **6)** a little / few / little car repairs that are inexpensive.

Ray works part time, so he has **7)** a lot of / many / much free time. He figures the parts for the car won't cost **8)** a lot of / many / few money. He only needs **9)** a few / a little / few parts. Ray will have to borrow the tools he needs from a friend because he doesn't have **10)** few / many / much car tools. If he spends **11)** a little / few / little time on his car every day, maybe an hour or two, he can save **12)** a lot of / many / much money, probably hundreds of dollars.

* break down: *to stop working*

Determiners and Pronouns

Read the story carefully. Then complete the sentences with one of the words in the box.

anybody / anything / anywhere, etc.	nobody / nothing / nowhere, etc.
one / ones	some / any
somebody / something / somewhere, etc.	this / that / these / those

I admire my friend Ken. He is very good natured. **1)** _Nothing_ bothers

him.* **2)** _____ seems very unusual to me because I know he is a very busy

person. I guess he is just one of **3)** _____ people who were born happy. I

don't know **4)** _____ who does not like Ken. He doesn't say bad

things about **5)** _____ , and **6)** _____ has anything bad to

say about him. In addition, he doesn't complain about **7)** _____

that happens.

Ken is always ready to help people – he is very thoughtful. If a family member or friend

needs to go **8)** _____ , Ken is always ready to give the person a ride. If

someone needs **9)** _____ , he tries to help them get it. And he never forgets

10) _____'s birthday.

It seems that Ken has **11)** _____ problems in his life, but, of course, he has

the same **12)** _____ as other people. But he doesn't spend **13)** _____

time complaining. Instead, he thinks about what he can do to solve the problem. How much

time does he spend feeling sorry for himself? **14)** _____! He is grateful for

everything. **15)** _____ is what makes Ken a special person.

  * nothing bothers him: *nothing is a problem for him; nothing worries him*

Use your own ideas to complete the sentences.

1. Most people *are honest* OR *have to work* _____ .
   Most people _____ .

2. Most of the people I know _____
   _____ .

3. Some doctors _____
   _____ .

4. _____ some of the _____
   _____ .

5. No parent should _____
   _____ .

6. None of my _____
   _____ .

7. A lot of people _____
   _____ .

8. _____ both my grandfathers _____
   _____ .

9. All politicians _____
   _____ .

10. All of my neighbors _____
    _____ .

11. _____ , but I didn't like either of them.

12. "_____ ,"
    asked _____ . "Neither," I said.

13. Everyone in my family _____ .

Old, nice, interesting, etc. (Adjectives)
Quickly, badly, suddenly, etc. (Adverbs)

Adjectives and Adverbs

Complete the sentences, keeping the same meaning.

1. There was a sudden change in the weather.
   The weather *changed suddenly*   .

2. My husband cooks well.
   My husband is a *good cook*   .

3. I'm not going to eat this apple. It has a strange taste.
   I'm not going to eat this apple. It tastes _____ .

4. Look at the used car carefully before you buy it.
   Take a _____ look at _____
   before you buy it.

5. Dave is a good worker but slow.
   Dave works _____ .

6. My brother was a good student.
   _____ did _____ in school.

7. The judge answered my question clearly and briefly.
   _____ gave a _____
   answer to _____ .

8. The mail is always late on Saturday.
   _____ comes _____ .

9. Patrick answered quietly but well.
   Patrick's answer was _____ .

10. I don't want to ride with Jenny. She drives recklessly.*
    Jenny is a _____ driver.

11. There was heavy rain yesterday afternoon.
    It rained _____ yesterday afternoon.

   * recklessly: *carelessly*

Old/older and expensive / more expensive
Older than . . . and more expensive than . . .

Use the words in parentheses to write sentences with *than*.

1. (summer / hot / spring) _Summer is hotter than spring._

2. (the Pyramids / famous / the Washington Monument) _The Pyramids are more famous than the Washington Monument._

3. (Mexico City / big / Lima) _____

4. (the Nile River / long / the Amazon) _____

5. (Tokyo / crowded / Nairobi) _____

6. (New York / close to Montreal / to Miami) _____

7. (Iceland / far north / England) _____

8. (Hawaii / has / nice weather / Alaska) _____

9. (Puerto Rico / has / bad rain storms / Egypt) _____

10. (Moscow / has / cold winters / London) _____

11. (Australia / large / New Zealand) _____

12. (the Petronas Towers in Malaysia / tall / the Sears Tower in Chicago) _____

Write questions that go with the answers. Use *as . . . as . . . .*

Questions	Answers
1. Do you *read as fast as your brother* _____ ?	No, my brother reads much faster than me.
2. Is France _____ ?	No, Canada is much bigger than France.
3. Has Ted _____ you?	No, I've lived here much longer than Ted.
4. Do you _____ ?	No, my mother gets up much earlier than me.
5. Are apples _____ ?	No, cherries are more expensive than apples.
6. Is baseball _____ ?	No, soccer is much more popular than baseball in the world.
7. Do _____ ?	No, my father works much harder than me.
8. _____	No, the flu is much worse than a cold.
9. _____	No, my brother goes out much more than my sister.
10. _____	No, doctors have more patients than dentists do.

NITS
9-90

Older than . . . and *more expensive than . . .*
Not as . . . as

Read the story. Then fill each blank with one word.

My friend Frank and I are trying to lose weight because we are heavier **1)** <u>*than*</u>

we were five years ago. Frank weighs a **2)** <u>*little*</u> more than I do – he's 185

pounds, and I'm 180 pounds. I'm the same height **3)** _____ Frank, and we are

almost the **4)** _____ age, 24 and 23. He gets **5)** _____ exercise

than I do, but I don't eat as much **6)** _____ he does. Neither of us is

7) _____ active as we were in high school. We sit **8)** _____ more

than before, and we walk and play sports **9)** _____ than before. The doctor

thinks we eat too many sweet and fattening foods*.

We are both trying to eat **10)** _____ fat, but it seems we like fattening food

more than we do food that's good for us. Frank is a **11)** _____ worse than me

in one way: He often has something sweet for dessert, but I don't eat dessert very often.

* fattening food: *a food that makes people fat when they eat a lot of it*

The oldest and *the most expensive*

Write sentences with superlatives about the three pets*. Use the words in parentheses. Give your own opinions.

cat

bird

fish

1. (quiet) *The fish is the quietest.*

2. (expensive to buy) *The bird is the most expensive to buy.*

3. (good swimmer) *The fish is the best swimmer.*

4. (noisy) _____

5. (interesting to watch) _____

6. (nice pet) _____

7. (easy to feed) _____

8. (popular pet) _____

9. (pleasant to hold) _____

10. (dangerous for children) _____

11. (pretty) _____

12. (hard to take along on vacation) _____

13. (difficult to take care of) _____

14. (good birthday present for a child) _____

* pets: *animals that people keep at home*

EXERCISE 103

Enough

Complete the conversations. Use *enough* with the words in parentheses. Add *to* or *for* where needed.

1. *A:* What did the doctor say?

   B: She said I don't *get enough sleep* _____ (get / sleep).

2. *A:* What did the doctor say?

   B: He said I don't *eat enough vegetables* _____ (eat / vegetables).

3. *A:* Shall we stop somewhere to eat before the movie?

   B: There isn't *enough time for us to eat* _____ (time / us / eat) before the movie.

4. *A:* Can you help me move this piano?

   B: I don't think I _____ (be / strong / move) the piano.

5. *A:* Did you go swimming in Florida?

   B: No, it wasn't _____ (warm / go swimming).

6. *A:* Ben doesn't play the guitar as well as he used to.

   B: You're right. He doesn't _____ (get / practice).

7. *A:* Could you please set the table for dinner?

   B: I can't. There aren't _____ (clean plates / everyone).

8. *A:* Do those shoes fit?

   B: Not really. They aren't _____ (big / me).

9. *A:* I heard Ben lost his job.

   B: Yes, I don't think he worked _____ (hard).

10. *A:* *(in a car)* We don't have _____ (gas / get) to Portland.

    B: You're right. We'd better stop and buy some.

11. *A:* Do you always bring work home?

    B: No, but I didn't have _____ (time / finish) this work at the office.

12. *A:* Is _____ (the soup / salty / you)?

    B: Yes, it's perfect.

UNITS
92-93

Enough
Too

A. Complete the sentences. Use *too*, *too much*, or *too many*. If needed, use *for*, *to*, and any other words.

1. Let's not sit here. (noisy) It <u>'s too noisy</u> .

2. Let's not sit here. (noise) There <u>'s too much noise</u> .

3. None of us did the homework. (difficult / us / do) It <u>was too difficult for us to do</u> .

4. I don't want to play tennis now. (hot / play) It _____ .

5. I didn't buy the shoes. (small / me) They _____ .

6. Frank can be very boring. (talk) He _____ .

7. I couldn't see the doctor today. (busy / see me) She _____ .

8. We couldn't drive up the mountain. (snow) There _____ .

9. I couldn't get tickets to the movie. (people) There _____ .

10. I never buy imported cheese. (cost) It _____ .

B. Complete the sentences with *too*, *too much*, *too many*, or *enough* and any other words that are necessary.

1. I can't use this suitcase. (small) It <u>is too small</u> .

2. Miles is a little lazy. (exercise) He <u>doesn't exercise enough</u> .

3. Arthur and Gwen plan to get married soon. (young / get married) Their families think
   they are _____ .

4. Rita has trouble sleeping. (coffee) She drinks _____ .

5. Gabriel is four. (little / play soccer) He _____ .

6. Do you need money? (money / your trip) Do you have _____ ?

7. I don't speak Japanese very well. (mistakes) I make _____ .

8. Only six hours a night? (get / sleep) You _____ .

REVIEW

Adjectives and Adverbs

Use your own ideas to write sentences with the words in parentheses. The <u>underlined</u> words are verbs, and sometimes you will need to put them in the correct form.

1. (good / angry / slowly) *If you are angry, it's a good idea to count to ten slowly before speaking.* OR *A good driver doesn't get angry when others drive slowly.*

2. (<u>do</u> / nervous / badly) _____

3. (<u>sound</u> / foreign) _____

4. (quickly / slow) _____

5. (<u>taste</u> / delicious / hot) _____

6. (<u>look</u> / surprised) _____

7. (quiet / well / early) _____

8. (<u>drive</u> / dangerous / carefully) _____

9. (<u>feel</u> / suddenly / tired) _____

10. (<u>look</u> / good / in blue) _____

11. (<u>speak</u> / softly / difficult / understand) _____

Complete the sentences, keeping the same meaning.

Superlative	Than / Not as . . . as
1. Mexico City is the biggest city in North and South America.	*Mexico City is bigger than* the other cities in North and South America.
2. *Ben is the tallest* child in his family.	Ben's brothers and sisters aren't as tall as he is.
3. This is _____ _____ I've ever had.	This job is more interesting than other jobs I've had.
4. Mrs. Reese is the busiest person I know.	_____ than any other person I know.
5. _____ _____ in town.	The other restaurants aren't as expensive as The Grill.
6. Mike's is the best barber shop in town.	The other barber shops aren't _____ _____ .
7. The Nile is the longest river in the world.	The Nile is _____ _____ than any other river.
8. Everest is the highest mountain in the world.	No other mountain is _____ _____ .
9. _____ _____ person I know.	Mrs. Johnson is more patient than anyone else I know.
10. Jupiter is the largest planet in the solar system.	_____ _____ any of the other planets.
11. That _____ _____ this year.	Other storms this year weren't as bad as that storm.
12. Eric bought _____ _____ in the store.	Eric's TV was cheaper than all the other TVs in the store.
13. I bought _____ _____ in the store.	My shoes were more expensive than all the other shoes in the store.

Adjectives and Adverbs

Read the story. Then complete the sentences with the correct form of the adjective in parentheses.

A Family Vacation

The Peters family drove to Quebec City from Toronto for a week's vacation last June. They had a long drive, but it wasn't 1) *as difficult* (difficult) as they expected. They left on a Saturday because they know traffic is often 2) *worse* (bad) on weekday mornings than on Saturday. They left Toronto 3) *later* (late) than they planned, but the road was still not 4) _____ (crowded) as on a weekday. Of course, when you travel with children, you have to stop a little 5) _____ (often), so they arrived in Quebec late. They went to their hotel, which was in an old building. It was 6) _____ (expensive) than some of the newer hotels, but the newer ones wouldn't have been 7) _____ (nice). The Peters thought that it was one of the 8) _____ (pretty) hotels they had ever stayed in.

Traveling with young children poses problems. The Peters children are only eight and five. Sometimes it can be difficult to eat out with children because they don't like 9) _____ (many) different kinds of food as adults do. The first night the Peters asked where the 10) _____ (close) restaurant was because they were too tired to go far. When you don't speak the language, it can be much 11) _____ (difficult) to order food in a restaurant. However, the Peters found that they were able to manage because most people spoke some English and the children were able to find food that they liked.

The family visited places outside like the zoo, the fort, and the Old City. These places were 12) _____ (interesting) for the children than museums. People told the Peters that the time of year they were there – early summer – was probably the 13) _____ (good) time to visit Quebec. People there said the weather was 14) _____ (warm) than usual for the time of year and it was 15) _____ (sunny) than normal. The family enjoyed themselves, and they all agreed it was the 16) _____ (nice) vacation they have ever had.

He speaks English very well. (Word Order)
Always/usually/often, etc. (Word Order)

Word Order

Put the words in order to make sentences. Some are questions.

1. (at a restaurant / order / I / never / fish)
   <u>*I never order fish at a restaurant.*</u>

2. (my new car / my sister / very much / doesn't like)
   _____

3. (both / work / Mark and Amy / in the same office)
   _____

4. (met / him / Samantha / last month / at a party)
   _____

5. (at a club / the Wymans / go dancing / every weekend / still)
   _____

6. (leave / in the kitchen / dirty dishes / you / do / overnight / ever?)
   _____

7. (met / you / have / already / my boss?)
   _____

8. (with her friends / on weekends / Clare / time to go out / has / seldom)
   _____

9. (still / buy / have to / some stamps / this afternoon / I / at the post office)
   _____

10. (the lights / at night / to turn off / you / sometimes / do / forget?)
    _____

11. (Fred / at home / eat / doesn't / dinner / after work / usually)
    _____

12. (are / both / my two uncles / police officers)
    _____

Still, yet, and already

Complete the conversations with *still*, *already*, or *yet* and the correct form of a verb.

1. *A:* *(on the phone)* Can I speak to Kathy?

   B: Sorry, she _is still_____ at work. She hasn't _come_____
   home _yet_____ .

2. *A:* I have some news to tell you about Kathy.

   B: If it's about her new job, she has _already told_____ me.

3. *A:* Do you _____ cards every week?

   B: No, we don't have time to play cards so often.

4. *A:* Here's a copy of my report.

   B: Thanks, but I _____ a copy in my briefcase.

5. *A:* Has the mail carrier _____ ?

   B: No, she doesn't come until the afternoon.

6. *A:* Have you _____ a job _____ ?

   B: No, I haven't found one. I'm _____ .

7. *A:* Have you _____ your parents about your accident
   _____ ?

   B: No, I'm afraid to tell them. It happened in their new car.

8. *A:* Is Angela coming with us to see the movie?

   B: No. She's _____ it.

9. *A:* *(at a party)* I want to say hello to your parents. Where are they?

   B: They _____ here _____ . But they're on their
   way, and they should be here soon.

10. *A:* We still have to wash the dishes before we go to bed.

    B: No, we don't. I've _____ them.

11. *A:* Have you changed jobs?

    B: No, I'm _____ in my father's store.

Give me that book! Give it to me!

A. Complete the conversations with a pronoun (*it, me, them, you*, etc.) + *to* or *for* followed by another pronoun.

1. *A:* Would you like more to eat? Some more potatoes?

   B: Yes, would you please pass _them to me_ ?

2. *A:* Did your sister get your letter?

   B: I suppose so. I sent _it to her_ last week.

3. *A:* Some friends of mine would like to see your new car.

   B: I could show _____ tomorrow if they're free.

4. *A:* These flowers are beautiful. Who are they for?

   B: For mom. Could you give _____ when she comes home?

5. *A:* Thank you for the gift. These bowls are beautiful. Where did you get them?

   B: I bought _____ on my trip to Japan.

6. *A:* Did you and Jeff buy this sofa when you got married?

   B: No. My parents got _____ .

7. *A:* I like your jacket.

   B: It's not mine. Someone lent _____ .

8. *A:* This juice is for the children.

   B: I'll give _____ .

B. Complete the sentences with the words in parentheses in the correct order.

1. I sent _my sister a postcard_ (a postcard / my sister).

2. They showed _____ (me / a picture of their baby).

3. I lent _____ (a cup of sugar / my neighbor).

4. They bought _____ (a car / their parents).

5. Could you get _____ (a newspaper / my father) when you go out?

Use your own ideas to write sentences with the words in parentheses. You can change the order of the words given.

1. (forget / never) <u>*My father never forgets to pay his bills.*</u>
   <u>OR *I have never forgotten my keys in the car.*</u>
   _____

2. (buy / me) <u>*My sister bought me a card for my birthday.*</u>
   _____

3. (be / usually) _____
   _____

4. (be / also) _____
   _____

5. (wear / still) _____
   _____

6. (lend / strangers) _____
   _____

7. (photos / show / us) _____
   _____

8. (go / rarely) _____
   _____

9. (be / yet) _____
   _____

10. (learn / already) _____
    _____

11. (on the weekend / breakfast / eat / in a restaurant) _____
    _____

UNIT
98

At 8 o'clock, on Monday, in April, etc.

A. Complete the sentences with *at*, *on*, or *in*. If no preposition is necessary, write *X*.

1. Beatrice started her new job *X*_____ last Monday. She'll tell us about it
   *on*_____ the weekend when she visits.

2. I can't see the dentist _____ this week or _____ next week, but I have
   an appointment _____ three weeks.

3. Aaron likes starting work _____ 5 A.M., but it was hard for him _____
   the beginning.

4. My birthday is _____ next Wednesday, but we're celebrating it _____
   today.

5. I try to exercise _____ every day, usually _____ the morning
   but sometimes _____ night.

B. Rewrite the second sentence with the words in parentheses. Use *in*, *on*, or *at* where necessary.

1. Today is March 21. My exam is on April 4.
   (next month) *My exam is next month.*_____

2. Today is March 21. My exam is on April 4.
   (two weeks) *My exam is in two weeks.*_____

3. It's 2 P.M. I have a coffee break in two hours.
   (4 P.M.) _____

4. I'm busy this afternoon. I'll take you to the bank early tomorrow.
   (the morning) _____

5. I have to study. We have quizzes on Thursdays.
   (every Thursday) _____

6. Hurry, it's 4:50. The bank closes at 5.
   (ten minutes) _____

From . . . to, until, since, and for

Complete the sentences, keeping the same meaning. Use the word in parentheses.

1. Alice lived in Brazil from 1992 to 1998.

   (for) Alice _lived in Brazil for six years_ .

2. Lily went to bed at midnight.

   (until) Lily _stayed up until midnight_ .

3. Les went to the gym early this morning, and he's still there.

   (since) Les has been at _____ .

4. I haven't worked since I moved here six weeks ago.

   (for) I haven't worked _____ .

5. I can take care of your baby, but I have to leave at two.

   (until) I _____ two.

6. Cindy had red hair when she was born, and she still has the same color hair.

   (since) Cindy has had red hair _____ .

7. When Charlie loses ten pounds, he'll stop exercising.

   (until) Charlie will exercise _____ .

8. Sam was an actor in New York for five years. He stopped acting in 2001.

   (from . . . to . . .) Sam was an actor _____ .

9. I worked at the computer all morning. Then I had lunch.

   (until) I worked _____ .

10. Helen moved to Philadelphia when she got married and she says she never wants to move away.

    (since) Helen has lived _____ .

11. Sylvia was married for five years. She got divorced in 2002.

    (from . . . to . . .) Sylvia was _____ .

EXERCISE 114

Before, after, during, and *while*

Complete the sentences, keeping the same meaning. Use the word in parentheses.

1. Passengers on an airplane have to fasten their seatbelts during takeoff and landing.

   (while) Passengers on an airplane *have to fasten their seatbelts while the airplane* takes off and lands.

2. Bob always checks his briefcase before he leaves for work.

   (before) Bob *always checks his briefcase before* _____ leaving for work.

3. After finishing my exercises, I take a shower.

   (after) _____ I _____ , I take a shower.

4. Mr. Riggan and his brother didn't speak to each other from 1982 to 1996.

   (for) Mr. Riggan and his brother _____ years.

5. Before going to bed, could you lock the doors?

   (before) Could you _____ you _____ ?

6. During the time they were neighbors, Mike and Sally never met.

   (while) _____ , Mike and Sally never met.

7. Students need to concentrate* while they are taking exams.

   (during) Students _____ exams.

8. I worked on the exam from nine to noon without a break.

   (for) I _____ without a break.

9. I always brush my teeth after I eat.

   (after) I _____ eating.

10. Margot got sick during dinner.

    (while) Margot _____ eating dinner.

11. Most people dream while they are asleep, but they may not remember their dreams.

    (during) Most people _____ the night, but they may not remember their dreams.

* concentrate: *to keep your attention on something*

In, at, and on (Places)

Read what the woman in the car is saying to the driver. Complete the sentences with *in*, *at*, or *on*.

"Gloria lives 1) _on_ this street. She lives 2) _____ a big white house.

I am sure that she doesn't live 3) _____ the middle of the block. I'm sure she lives

4) _____ the end of the block. In fact, I think her house is right 5) _____

the corner. There are some nice bushes and a birdbath 6) _____ the front yard.

The family's last name is 7) _____ the front door of the house. Gloria and her family

live 8) _____ the first floor. Let's see if anyone is 9) _____ home. She might be

10) _____ work, and the children are probably 11) _____ school. But we can

leave a note to say we're sorry her husband is 12) _____ the hospital. The poor

man! He had an accident when he was 13) _____ his motorcycle. I know because I saw

the story 14) _____ the newspaper this morning. You couldn't miss it – it was right

15) _____ the top of page one. How did the accident happen? Well, they say a

driver 16) _____ an old car didn't stop 17) _____ the traffic light.

Imagine! That driver should be 18) _____ jail. What 19) _____ the world

was he thinking?

"Well, you're not talking very much. Let's hurry to Gloria's – I have to be 20) _____

the doctor's in an hour. Actually, can you drive me there after our visit to Gloria's? My son is

21) _____ a football game, and I can call him from the doctor's office to pick me

up*. We're having dinner 22) _____ my sister's tonight, and she lives 23) _____

the next town 24) _____ a busy street. You can't imagine the noise! Well, I just love

talking to you. You're such a good listener. I'm glad we're 25) _____ your car – it's easier

to talk that way."

* pick (someone) up: *to take someone by car from one place to another*

In, at, and *on* (Places)

Complete the questions with prepositions. Then write sentences to answer the questions.

1. Would you rather live __*in*__ a cold country or __*in*__ a warm country?
    __*I'd rather live in a warm country than in a cold country.*__

2. Would you rather live _____ the first floor of a building or _____ the fortieth floor?
    _____

3. Would you rather spend time _____ a concert or _____ the beach?
    _____

4. Would you rather be _____ college or _____ elementary school?
    _____

5. Would you rather work _____ your desk or exercise _____ the gym?
    _____

6. Would you rather sleep _____ a bed or _____ the floor?
    _____

7. Would you rather live _____ a big city, _____ a small town, or _____ the country?
    _____

8. Would you rather take a long trip _____ a train or _____ a car?
    _____

9. Would you rather stay _____ a hotel or _____ a friend's?
    _____

10. In nice weather, would you rather eat _____ the dining room or _____ the balcony?
    _____

11. Would you rather spend free time _____ a park or _____ a museum?
    _____

12. Would you rather swim _____ a pool or _____ the ocean?
    _____

EXERCISE 117

To, in, and *at* (Places)

Complete the sentences about the picture. Use the words in parentheses. Use *to, in,* and *at* where necessary. Put the verb in an appropriate form.

1. Mrs. Ramos *is at the mall* _____ (be / the mall).

2. She was *at a department store* _____ (be / a department store).

3. She didn't _____ (go / the bank).

4. She _____ (go / home now).

5. When she _____ (get / home), she'll work in her home office.

6. The police officer _____ (arrive / the mall) five minutes ago.

7. He is _____ (sit / his car).

8. The police car _____ (be / the parking lot).

9. The police officer _____ (return / the police station) in an hour.

10. The girl didn't _____ (go / school) today.

11. She _____ (get / the mall) a few minutes ago.

12. She _____ (come / the mall) to meet her friends.

13. Her parents think she _____ (be / school).

14. She might be in trouble when she _____ (get / home).

**Look at the picture. Correct the sentences by changing the underlined parts.
Use the words in the box, and any other words that you need.**

| above | below | by | in front of | next to | on the right |
| across from | between | in back of | in the middle | on the left | under |

1. The young man is sitting <u>across from</u> the young woman.

   The young man is sitting next to the young woman.

2. He is holding flowers <u>next to</u> the table.

   _____

3. The couple's table is <u>above</u> the window.

   _____

4. The big table is <u>on the left.</u>

   _____

5. There is a light <u>on</u> the big table.

   _____

6. The children are sitting <u>next to</u> each other.

   _____

7. There are two small tables <u>on the right.</u>

   _____

EXERCISE CONTINUES ▶ ▶

8. There is a mouse <u>on</u> one of the tables.

_____

9. The cook is standing <u>in front of</u> the waiter.

_____

10. The busboy* is <u>between</u> the cook and the waiter.

_____

11. A woman is checking her makeup <u>next to</u> the mirror.

_____

12. The mirror is <u>in</u> the restrooms.

_____ the restrooms.

13. The telephone is <u>in back of</u> the restrooms.

_____

  * busboy: _a person who works in a restaurant and helps waiters doing tasks such as carrying dishes or cleaning tables_

Up, over, through, etc.

These sentences don't make sense*. Rewrite the sentences, correcting the underlined parts.

1. We walked from <u>the restaurant</u> to <u>the gas station</u> to eat lunch.
   We walked from the gas station to the restaurant to eat lunch.

2. I always <u>put</u> the clean dishes <u>in</u> the dishwasher.
   I always take the clean dishes out of the dishwasher.

3. Do you think I should hang this picture <u>below</u> the sofa?
   _____

4. Don't <u>take</u> your feet <u>off</u> the sofa. You'll make it dirty.
   _____

5. When I walked <u>into</u> the house, I felt a light rain.
   _____

6. Don't get <u>in</u> the car here – there's too much traffic. Wait until I park the car.
   _____

7. We walked <u>down</u> the hill to the house at the top.
   _____

8. Water freezes when the temperature is <u>above</u> zero degrees Celsius.
   _____

9. We sat <u>over</u> a big tree and had a picnic.
   _____

10. You should turn on your car lights when you drive <u>over</u> a tunnel.
    _____

11. If you're warm, why don't you jump <u>out of</u> the pool?
    _____

* make sense: *to be reasonable and logical*

EXERCISE CONTINUES ▶ ▶

12. The thief ran <u>into</u> the police station to escape.

_____

13. *(on the phone)* My apartment is on the fifth floor. Be careful when you walk <u>down</u> the stairs.

_____

14. The Smiths are <u>coming from</u> Australia next week. They've never been there before.

_____

15. I had to drive <u>into</u> the hospital four times before I found a parking place.

_____

16. The door is locked. Let's go in the house <u>past</u> the window.

_____

17. You can't get to San Francisco if you don't drive <u>through</u> this bridge.

_____

18. We didn't notice the barber shop even though we walked <u>into</u> it three times.

_____

19. Let's take our shoes off and walk <u>past</u> the beach.

_____

20. <u>Put</u> the dishes <u>in</u> the cabinet. It's time to set the table* for dinner.

_____

* set the table: *to put dishes on the table before a meal*

**Complete the sentences with the words in parentheses and *on, at, by, with,
without*, or *about*.**

1. My brother can help you. He knows *a lot about computers* (a lot / computers).

2. This meat is very tough. I can't cut _____ (it / this knife).

3. Mrs. Jordan is old fashioned. She doesn't like _____
   (young men / long hair).

4. Do you have any _____ (books / Mark Twain)? I love his stories.

5. I'm sorry you had to come back home. But how could you _____
   (leave home / your briefcase)?

6. Do you have _____ (any questions / the lesson)?

7. It's difficult to speak _____ (a foreign language / the phone).

8. The Chinese class is being taught _____ (a new teacher).

9. We will have to open this package _____ (scissors).

10. Our teacher says we must write _____ (our homework / a pen).

11. Is there _____ (anything good / TV)?

12. Is this painting _____ (a famous artist)?

13. Did you hear _____ (the accident / the radio)?

14. _____ (what age) can people drive in your country?

15. Do you go to work _____ (car / or / foot)?

16. Would you like your tea _____ or _____ (sugar)?

17. If you go _____ (bike), you won't get there _____ (time).

Afraid of, good at, etc. (Adjective + Preposition)
At -ing, with -ing, etc. (Preposition + *-ing*)

Complete the sentences with a word or phrase from the box and the necessary preposition. Change the form of words if necessary.

the accident	big animals	count money all day	do math problems	Gloria
go with us	~~her~~	him	his sister	me
pay bills	people	~~spend money~~	you	

1. Anita is a little unhappy today. Be nice _to her_ .

2. You can't go out to most places without _spending money_ .

3. We never go to the zoo. My little boy is afraid _____ .

4. Why isn't Sue talking to you? Is she angry _____ ?

5. There's no place to sit in the restaurant. It's full _____ .

6. You know the man I'm talking about. He's married _____ .

7. Please thank your father for the ride home. It was very kind _____ .

8. We're going to drive to Toronto next weekend. Are you interested _____ _____ ?

9. I'm going to quit my job at the bank. I'm tired _____ .

10. Michelle's brother will surprise you. He looks very different _____ .

11. Poor Tina got a letter from the electric company today because she owes money. She's not very good _____ .

12. I'm sorry. I can't help you with the homework. I'm bad _____ .

13. I'm sorry _____ . Did you get hurt?

14. *A:* Is your father angry because of your job?
    B: Yes, he's mad _____ for losing it.

Listen to . . . , look at . . . , etc. (Verb + Preposition)

Complete the description of the conversations. Use the verb in parentheses in the correct form and the correct preposition. Not all sentences need prepositions.

1. *Fiona:* What are you doing with your ear to the door?

   Ben: Shhh. I'm trying to hear what my brother is saying to his girlfriend.

   Ben is *listening to his brother's* _____ conversation. (listen)

2. *Roger:* The tie is beautiful! Thank you so much!

   His grandmother: You're welcome. I'm glad you like it.

   Roger *thanked his grandmother for* _____ the tie. (thank)

3. *Adam:* Have you seen my keys anywhere?

   John: No. Did you look in your car?

   Adam _____ his keys. (look)

4. *Ted:* Will you be here at Christmas?

   Sam: I'm not sure. I might go to Las Vegas.

   Sam _____ to Las Vegas. (think)

5. *Sarah:* Do you want to go to see a movie with me?

   Rosa: Maybe. If it's a movie I like.

   Rosa might go a movie with Sarah, but it _____ the movie. (depend)

6. *Tim:* How's Martin? Is he still in Africa?

   Mary Jo: I have no idea. I haven't heard anything.

   Martin hasn't _____ them. (write)

7. *Alice:* Do you have David's telephone number at work?

   Maria: Yes, I have it in my address book.

   Alice wants _____. (call)

8. *Aunt Hilary:* I'll stay home with the baby so you can go shopping.

   Sylvia: Thanks. I appreciate it.

   Aunt Hilary is going _____ the baby. (take care)

NITS
-103

Prepositions

Use your own ideas to write sentences with the words in parentheses. Add necessary prepositions *(in, at, on, from . . . to, until, since, for, before, after, during,* **or** *while).*

1. (5 o'clock / morning / bed) *Most people are in bed at 5 o'clock in the morning.*
   OR   I was asleep in bed at 5 o'clock this morning.

2. (married / many years) _____

3. (Friday mornings / the supermarket / my country) _____

4. (the weekend / home / midnight) _____

5. (two weeks / call) _____

6. (be back / Monday) _____

7. (brush / teeth / going to bed) _____

8. (waiting for a friend / study) _____

9. (9 A.M. to 2 P.M.) _____

10. (eat / watch a movie) _____

11. (travel / bicycle) _____

Look at the picture and read the story. Then complete the sentences with the correct prepositions (*next to, under, in back of, up, over, through, on, at, by, with, about,* etc.). **If no preposition is needed, write X.**

FRONT   BACK

A Break-in*

Someone broke into the Martins' house yesterday. They were away **1)** ___on___

vacation. I know **2)** _____ it because I talked **3)** _____ Mrs. Kahn,

the Martins' neighbor **4)** _____ the right, yesterday afternoon and she told me the

whole story. The burglar* entered the house **5)** _____ a back window. It seems

he climbed **6)** _____ the fence that goes all the way **7)** _____ the

Martins' backyard. The Kahns and the Garcias, who live **8)** _____ the

Martins, were home but did not hear or see anything. In fact, it seems the Martins always

leave a key **9)** _____ the rug by the back door of the house for the children to

use. But the burglar didn't find that key.

The break-in probably happened about 10 A.M. How do I know that? According to Mrs.

Kahn, a neighbor was walking **10)** _____ the Martins' house at that time, and

* break-in: *entering a house by breaking a window or a door to steal things*
* burglar: *a person who steals things from a house*

EXERCISE CONTINUES ▶ ▶

she saw a car parked 11) _____ the street 12) _____ the Martins'
house. A short time later, she saw a man 13) _____ short hair drive
away in the same car 14) _____ 50 or 60 miles per hour. She looked
15) _____ the Martins' house, saw that the front door was open, and called
16) _____ the police.

Strangely, nothing was stolen. Evidently, the burglar was interested only 17) _____
money and jewelry, which he didn't find in the house. He left 18) _____
taking anything. But he took a lot of things 19) _____ the cabinets and dressers
while he was looking 20) _____ things to steal.

The house was a mess. This had never happened 21) _____ the Martins before, so
of course they were upset when they came home last night. At the same time, they felt lucky
that nothing was stolen. And it was very nice 22) _____ their neighbors to help
them put the house back in order.

Now the Martins are thinking 23) _____ getting a dog, which the children
think is a great idea. We are all sorry 24) _____ the break-in, but you hear
so much 25) _____ crime these days 26) _____ the
radio and 27) _____ TV. I think we all have to be better 28) _____
taking care 29) _____ our neighbors and neighborhoods.

EXERCISE 125

Go in, fall off, run away, etc. (Two-Word Verbs)

Two-Word Verbs

Complete the story. Use the verbs in the box in the correct form.

come back	come back	come in	drive off	get along	get in	~~get up~~	go on
go away	grow up	keep on	look out	run away	stand up		

Ding dong. Someone was at my door at 7 A.M. on a Saturday morning. I **1)** <u>*got up*</u>
and went to the window and **2)** _____ . There were two police officers at the door.
"Do you mind if we **3)** _____ and ask you a few questions? Your neighbor, Tim
Barnes, has disappeared," the police said. "Maybe he is **4)** _____ from something, or
maybe he has just **5)** _____ for a while. Do you have any idea where he is?"

"No, I have no idea," I said. "Doesn't his wife have an idea where he might be?"

The police **6)** _____ with their story. "The last time his wife saw Tim was a week
ago when he **7)** _____ his car and **8)** _____ without saying
anything. Do you know if Tim and his wife had any problems?" asked one of the police
officers, who looked at his watch.

"I really don't know Tim and his wife very well, officer. But you could ask Tim's family and
friends. Tim **9)** _____ in this town. There are lots of people who know him here."

"We have already talked to his parents. Do you know if Tim had problems with anyone in
the neighborhood?" asked the same police officer, again glancing at his watch.

"No, as far as I know, Tim **10)** _____ with everyone. He is a very friendly guy," I
said. Then the officer who **11)** _____ looking at his watch ended our conversation
suddenly. He said, "Thank you. If you remember anything at all, please give us a call."

"I will. I feel sorry for his family. Do you think he'll **12)** _____ ?" I asked.

"People usually do. If he wasn't in any trouble, he will probably be back soon." Then the
two police officers **13)** _____ and left.

The next day, Tim **14)** _____ home. It seems he and his wife had fought* about
something, and he had left in a moment of anger and didn't tell anyone where he was. They
were both very happy when he returned, however.

* fought: *past participle of* fight

Put on your shoes and put your shoes on (Two-Word Verbs)

Complete the conversations. Use the correct form of the two-word verbs in parentheses and *it, him, them*, etc.

1. *A:* Does your father know Vancouver?

   B: No, I'm going to _show him around_ (show around) tomorrow.

2. *Child:* I don't want to play with these toys anymore.

   Father: Why don't you _____ (put away), and I'll read you a story?

3. *Customer:* These shoes say 47. What size is that in American sizes?

   Salesperson: Size 12, I think. Why don't you _____ (try on)?

4. *A:* What does "sanitarium" mean?

   B: I have no idea. _____ (look up) and tell me.

5. *A:* These library books are due* today.

   B: Yes, I'm going to _____ (take back) after lunch.

6. *A:* Do you still have yesterday's newspaper?

   B: No, I _____ (throw away) this morning.

7. *A:* The children are sleeping.

   B: Yes, let's not _____ (wake up).

8. *A:* Those old buildings are very pretty.

   B: It's a shame the city is going to _____ (tear down) for the new highway.

9. *A:* Thanks for the tools. I'll _____ (bring back) tomorrow.

   B: That's fine.

10. *A:* Does Don still play golf every day?

    B: No, he _____ (give up). He now goes swimming every day.

* due: *expected to be returned*

And, but, or, so, and *because*

Answer the questions with the words in parentheses and *and, but, or, so,* or *because*. Use appropriate verb forms.

1. What did Jeremy do yesterday? (play golf / go shopping at the mall)
   He played golf and went shopping at the mall.

2. What did his sister do? (play golf with him / not go shopping)
   She played golf with him, but she didn't go shopping.

3. Why didn't Jill go shopping with her brother? (not go / not like the mall)
   She didn't go shopping with her brother because she doesn't like the mall.

4. Why did Jeremy go shopping? (go shopping / need new clothes)
   _____

5. What did he do at the mall? (buy new pants / look at shoes)
   _____

6. Why didn't he get new shoes? (not fit / not get any)
   The shoes _____ .

7. Does he have to wear a jacket to work? (can wear a jacket / can wear a shirt and tie)
   _____

8. Why does he need new clothes? (start a new job last week / his old clothes not be very nice)
   _____

9. Does he like his job? (like the work / not know the other people very well yet)
   _____

10. What is his schedule at work? (can work ten hours a day four days a week / can work eight hours a day five days a week)
    _____
    _____

11. Does he get a vacation? (be new / not get a vacation for six months)
    _____
    _____

When . . .

Complete the conversations with the words in parentheses. Use any other words that are necessary.

1. *A:* How long has Ann lived here?

   B: She moved here _after she finished college_____ (after / finish college).

2. *A:* Can I help you with something?

   B: Yes, _before we go out_____ (before / go out), we have to close all the windows.

3. *A:* How long have you had this car?

   B: We bought it _____ (when / we / have the baby).

4. *A:* Is this package for me?

   B: Yes, it came _____ (while / you / be away).

5. *A:* How long will you stay with your grandfather?

   B: I really can't leave him _____ (until / be better).

6. *A:* Do you have my home address?

   B: Yes. I'll send you a postcard _____ (when / get to Moscow).

7. *A:* Mom, can I drive the car to the store?

   B: Absolutely not. You won't do any driving _____
   _____ (before / get a driver's license).

8. *A:* Should I turn the radio down?

   B: Yes, please. I can't talk on the phone _____
   _____ (while / the radio / play).

9. *A:* Do you want to go to the movies with us?

   B: No, thanks. _____
   _____ (when / be tired), I can't enjoy a movie.

10. *A:* Can you believe Al shaved his head?

    B: I didn't believe it _____ (until / see it).

If we go . . . , If you see . . . , etc.

A. Complete the conversations with the words in parentheses and any others that are necessary. Use the correct form of the verbs.

1. *A:* Why do we have to hurry?

   B: If we don't hurry, <u>*we'll miss our plane*</u> (miss / our plane).

2. *A:* Are we going on a hike tomorrow?

   B: We can go if <u>*the weather is nice*</u> (the weather / be / nice).

3. *A:* I feel terrible. Maybe I should stay home from work.

   B: Good idea. You'll feel better if _____

   _____ (stay / in bed).

4. *A:* Can we take a break now? I'm tired.

   B: _____ (not / finish / our work) if we stop now.

5. *A:* Can you help me move next week?

   B: I can help you if _____ (not / have to work).

6. *A:* Do you think Andy will be angry that I can't go to his party?

   B: No. If you explain, _____ (understand).

B. Complete the conversations. Use *when* or *if*.

1. *A:* When is your brother coming to visit?

   B: I don't know yet. <u>*I'll tell you when I know*</u> (tell you / I know).

2. *A:* What do you think of that used car?

   B: You'll _____ (be sorry / buy that car).

3. *A:* How's the weather today?

   B: Cold. You'll _____

   _____ (be more comfortable / wear a jacket).

4. *A:* Does your daughter drive yet?

   B: Not yet. She _____

   _____ (get a driver's license / be 16).

If I had . . . , If we went . . . , etc.

Complete the conversations.

1. *A:* You're studying a foreign language, aren't you?

   B: No, I'm not. *If I could study a foreign language* , I'd learn German.

2. *A:* Would you lend me your library card.

   B: Sorry. I *would lend it to you* if I knew where it was.

3. *A:* Is the weather nice?

   B: No. If it _____ , we could go for a walk.

4. *A:* Do you have Tom's address?

   B: Sorry, I don't. I'd give it to you _____ it.

5. *A:* Do you think Ann will pass her driving test?

   B: Probably not, but I think _____ it if she got more practice driving.

6. *A:* Can you play a musical instrument?

   B: No, but I'd be happier with myself _____ .

7. *A:* Can't your daughter drive you to work?

   B: No, she can't. _____ , I wouldn't have to walk.

8. *A:* Do you think our team will win five games this season?

   B: No, but I think _____ more often if we practiced more often together.

9. *A:* Can you take care of my son tomorrow?

   B: No. I'm sorry. I can't. If I weren't working, _____ .

10. *A:* Are you going to the store again?

    B: I have to. _____ if we didn't need milk.

EXERCISE 131

UNITS
113-
114

If we go . . . , If you see . . . , etc.
If I had . . . , If we went . . . , etc.

Check (✔) the sentence that is similar in meaning to the first one.

1. I wouldn't eat that if I were you.

   ✔ a. Don't eat that.

   ___ b. You can eat it, but I don't want to.

   ___ c. You don't need that. I'll eat it.

2. If Josh did his homework, he'd get good grades.

   ___ a. Josh used to get good grades.

   ___ b. Josh always does his homework, and he gets good grades.

   ___ c. Josh doesn't do his homework, and his grades aren't good.

3. Sheila will be sorry if she marries Al.

   ___ a. She won't marry Al.

   ___ b. She shouldn't marry Al.

   ___ c. She is going to marry Al.

4. I wouldn't call you this late if this wasn't important.

   ___ a. I have something important to tell you.

   ___ b. I know you stay up late, so I know you won't mind this call.

   ___ c. It's not very important – I'll call you later.

5. Your mother will be disappointed if you forget her birthday for a second time.

   ___ a. Your mother is going to be disappointed again.

   ___ b. Remember your mother's birthday.

   ___ c. Don't forget your mother's birthday again.

6. If you fail the driving test, you can take it again.

   ___ a. You will have to take the test again.

   ___ b. I don't think you will fail the test.

   ___ c. You might fail the driving test, but you'll have a chance to take it again.

7. If you want these magazines, I won't throw them away.

   ___ a. I want to keep these magazines.

   ___ b. I'm not going to throw the magazines away.

   ___ c. Do you want the magazines? Then I won't throw them away.

8. I wouldn't take these pills if they didn't help me.

   ___ a. I will continue to take the pills because they do me some good.

   ___ b. I won't take the pills anymore because they don't help me.

   ___ c. I have never taken these pills.

9. If Emily weren't sick, she would be at the party.

   ___ a. She wasn't sick, and she was at the party.

   ___ b. She was sick, and she wasn't at the party.

   ___ c. She is sick, and so she isn't at the party.

If we go . . . , If you see . . . , etc.
If I had . . . , If we went . . . , etc.

Use your own ideas to complete these sentences.

1. If I learn English very well, _I will be happy_ .
   If I learn English very well, _my parents will be proud of me_ .
   If I learn English very well, _my boss will give me a better job_ .
   If I learn English very well, _____ .

2. I would go to a lawyer _if I had a legal problem_ .
   I would go to a lawyer _____ .

3. If you spend too much money, _____ .

4. My family would not be happy _____ .

5. I don't mind if people _____ .

6. On my next vacation, I will visit _____ if
   _____ .

7. If there were no money in the world, _____ .

8. Most people would be happier if _____ .

9. My friends will have a party if _____ .

10. If I can, _____ .

11. If I could, _____ .

12. If you are late for class, _____ .

13. It isn't a problem if I _____ .

14. I wouldn't go to the doctor _____ .

15. When it is cloudy, _____ .

A person who . . . and a thing that / which . . . (Relative Clauses)

Make one sentence from two. Put a sentence from the box after the underlined wor

She can speak many languages.	The bird flew in the window.
✔ It is close to my apartment.	It flows through London.
✔ The people have the same first and last names.	They have borders with the United States.
The pen was on my desk.	They are marked fragile*.
He or she helps people with legal problems.	He said he could speak thirteen languages.

1. The <u>service station</u>ᴧrepairs cars on Sundays. *The service station which is close to*
   my apartment repairs cars on Sundays. OR *The service station that . . .*

2. There are many <u>people</u>ᴧin the phone book.
   There are many people *who have the same first and last names* in the phone book.

3. Did you take the <u>pen</u>ᴧ?
   Did you take the pen _____ ?

4. You should carry the <u>boxes</u>ᴧvery carefully.
   _____ very carefully.

5. The <u>bird</u>ᴧwas hard to catch.
   _____

6. I have an intelligent <u>friend</u>ᴧ.
   _____

7. A lawyer is a <u>professional</u>ᴧ.
   _____

8. The <u>man</u>ᴧwas a liar.
   _____

9. The <u>river</u>ᴧis called the Thames.
   _____

10. The <u>countries</u>ᴧare Canada and Mexico.
    _____

*fragile: *easily broken; delicate*

The people we met and *the hotel you stayed at* (Relative Clauses)

Make one sentence from the two sentences in parentheses. Put the second sentence after the underlined word. Do not use *who*, *which*, or *that*.

1. (Do you remember the nice <u>man</u>_∧_? We met the man at the party.)

    Do you remember the nice man we met at the party?

2. (The <u>man</u>_∧_ was wearing a gray suit. I'm talking about that man.)

    The man I'm talking about was wearing a gray suit.

3. (He told me about a <u>daughter</u>_∧_. He hasn't seen his daughter for a long time.)

    He told me about _____

    _____ .

4. (His daughter married a <u>doctor</u>_∧_. She met the doctor in a hospital in a village in India.)

    _____

    _____

5. (The <u>village</u>_∧_ is in the high mountains. His daughter and her husband live in the village.)

    _____

    _____

6. (They have <u>two children</u>_∧_. The man has seen the children only a few times.)

    _____

    _____

7. (The children go to a <u>school</u>_∧_ in New Delhi. They love the school.)

    _____

    _____

8. (The <u>man</u>_∧_ is going to visit his daughter and her family soon. We talked to the man at the party.)

    _____

    _____

EXERCISE 135

UNITS
115-
116

A person who... and *a thing that/which...*
The people we met and *the hotel you stayed at* (Relative Clauses)

Complete the sentences. Use information from the first sentence. Do not use
who, which **and** *that* **if they are not necessary.**

1. Hugh started a new job last week.
   Hugh doesn't like the job *he started last week* .

2. You and Oliver had lunch at a new restaurant last week.
   Oliver, what's the name of the restaurant *where we had lunch last week*
   OR *we had lunch at last week* ?

3. This woman flew around the world a long time ago.
   I can't remember the name of the woman *who flew around the world a long time ago* .

4. Liz works at a high school.
   Liz, what's the name of the high school _____ ?

5. Vanessa bought a lot of groceries this morning.
   Vanessa, where did you put the groceries _____ ?

6. That old building was destroyed last year.
   I miss the old building _____ .

7. We were looking at some photos.
   I don't know where I put the photos _____ .

8. This woman lived next door to us in Tokyo.
   We got a letter from the woman _____ .

9. We waited two hours for a bus.
   The bus _____ never came.

10. I am taking classes this semester.
    The classes _____ meet twice a week.

11. We stayed at a hotel on vacation.
    The hotel _____ had a swimming pool.

NITS
'11-
'16

Conjunctions and Clauses

Use your own ideas to complete the sentences.

1. If I can't _visit my grandmother today, I'll see her tomorrow for sure_ .

   If I can't _____ .

2. If I couldn't _____ .

3. Because I don't _____ .

4. _____ , so they stopped.

5. When the weather is nice, _____ .

6. If the weather is nice, _____ .

7. My family will probably _____ if _____ .

8. My family would never _____ if _____ .

9. _____ a friend who _____ .

10. _____ a person I _____ .

11. _____ something which _____ .

12. _____ something we _____ .

13. _____ , or we won't have any.

14. _____ a city where _____ .

15. _____ the city where _____ .

16. In my free time, I do things which _____ .

17. I don't like places which _____ .

18. I don't like places where _____ .

19. She asked me for my phone number, but _____ .

20. _____ and laughed.

EXERCISE 137

UNITS
111-
116

REVIEW
Conjunctions and Clauses

Read the story. Then complete the sentences with the words in parentheses and any other words you need. Put the verbs in the correct form.

One Hundred Years Old

May had her one hundredth birthday yesterday. She lives alone now because her husband is dead. She misses him, but she isn't lonely. She could live with one of her children, but she likes living in her own house. One of her great-grandchildren might move in with her; she likes that idea very much. For May, every day is busy, and every day is new.

She talks about the past, but she also talks about what she wants to do in the future. She is saving money to visit China. Her children want to buy her a ticket, but she won't allow them to. She is a very independent woman.

May is optimistic*. At 100, she has had her share of problems*. Her life has not been easy. But the problems never make her lose hope about life and the future.

May is very sociable*. Although she lives alone, she enjoys being with people: friends, neighbors, children, grandchildren, and great-grandchildren. Every day there are people at her house, and she is always ready to sit down, talk, and eat with them.

May is active. She still takes care of her house and garden. She grows a few vegetables and a lot of beautiful flowers. You can be sure she will be in her garden at seven tomorrow morning unless it rains.

May is a good example for all of us.

1. (husband still alive / not be alone)

    If _May's husband were still alive, she wouldn't be alone_ .

2. (be happy / a great-grandchild move in)

    May will be happy if _a great-grandchild moves in with her_ .

3. (think only about the past a lot / not be so happy)

    If _____ .

* optimistic: *looking at the positive side of things*
* her share of problems: *a number of problems; as many problems as other people*
* sociable: *friendly; liking to be with people*

EXERCISE CONTINUES ▶ ▶

4. (save enough money / go to China)

    When _____ .

5. (not work in the garden / it rain)

    _____ when _____ .

6. (be in her garden at 7 A.M. tomorrow / not rain)

    _____ if _____ .

7. (not be busy and active / not be happy)

    If _____ .

8. (lose hope / not be happy)

    If _____ .

9. (probably not have as many friends / not be so sociable)

    _____ if _____ .

Answer Key

Exercise 1

2. 's (is) hot
3. 're (are) very tall
4. He's (He is) hungry.
5. They're (They are) interested in cars.
6. He's (He is) thirsty.
7. She's (She is) tired.
8. They're (They are) happy.
9. She's (She is) angry.
10. It's (It is) heavy.

Exercise 2

2. Poland aren't (are not) warm countries
3. Diamonds are expensive.
   Tea and a newspaper aren't (are not) expensive.
4. Vancouver and Toronto are in Canada.
   Atlanta isn't (is not) in Canada.
5. I'm (I am) married. *or* I'm (I am) single.
   I'm (I am) not married. *or* I'm (I am) not single.
6. Santiago, Lima, and Buenos Aires are in South America.
   Madrid isn't (is not) in South America.
7. Eggs, butter, and sugar are necessary for a cake.
   Pepper isn't (is not) necessary for a cake.
8. 're (are) from another country *or* 're (are) from Brazil.
   're not (We are not)/We aren't (are not) from Brazil. *or* We're not (We are not)/We aren't (are not) from another country.

Exercise 3

3. Is your friend from Russia?
4. How are your parents?
5. Where is Linda's apartment?
6. Are you tired?
7. How much is this postcard?
8. What color is Julia's hair?
9. Are your teachers nice?
10. How old are you?
11. Why are you angry with me?
12. Who are those people?
13. What are their names?
14. Am I right?

Exercise 4

2. a. 's playing (is playing) soccer
   b. isn't (is not) doing her homework
3. a. aren't eating (are not eating) at home
   b. 're having (are having) dinner in a restaurant
4. a. is sitting in the park
   b. He's not working (He is not working) now.

5. a. 's not writing (is not writing) a letter
   b. She's studying (She is studying) English.
6. a. isn't fixing (is not fixing) the car
   b. She's washing (She is washing) the car.

Exercise 5

2. Where are you staying?
3. Are you traveling with somebody?
4. Are you seeing other friends here?
5. How are you enjoying my town?
6. How are you getting around town?
7. Are you visiting famous places here?
8. Are you interested in art museums?
9. Where are you now?
10. What are you doing now?

Exercise 6

1. She doesn't enjoy (does not enjoy) new places.
   She doesn't know (does not know) other languages.
   She doesn't like (does not like) to take airplanes.
2. doesn't eat (does not eat) healthy food
   He doesn't sleep (does not sleep) enough.
   He smokes a lot.
3. don't make (do not make) a lot of money
   They don't live (do not live) in a very nice place.
   They have boring jobs.
4. like to be with people
   I don't talk (do not talk) about others behind their back.
   I listen to others' problems.
5. listen to your employees
   You work hard.
   You don't get (do not get) angry often.

Exercise 7

2. it snow a lot there in the winter
3. do you do there
4. Do you teach French as a second language?
5. Do children in Quebec study French?
6. Do people in Quebec speak French?
7. many students do you have in your class
8. Do many tourists visit Quebec City?
9. Do you teach in the summer?
10. Do you take a vacation every year?
11. Where do you usually go?

Exercise 8

A.

2. a. Yes, she does.
   b. No, she isn't.
   c. No, she isn't.
   d. She's swimming (She is swimming).
   e. She fixes cars. *or* She's (She is) a mechanic.
3. a. No, they aren't.
   b. Yes, they do.
   c. No, they aren't.
   d. They're cooking (They are cooking).
   e. Yes, they do.
4. Answers will vary.
   Sample answers:
   a. Yes, I am.
   b. Yes, I am.
   c. No, I don't.
   d. I play soccer.

B.

2. a. What does Seth do?
   b. Is he writing a story?
   c. What is he doing?
   d. Where is he sitting?
   e. Does he use a computer for work?
3. a. Does Luke cook?
   b. Is he cooking?
   c. Does he play computer games?
   d. What does he do?
4. a. Is Emily laughing?
   b. Is she eating?
   c. Does she speak English?
   d. Does she look happy?

Exercise 9

A.

Answers will vary.
Sample answers:
2. I have a lot of friends.
3. I don't have a part-time job.
4. My brother has an earache.
5. My sister doesn't have a lot of free time.

B.

Answers will vary.
Sample answers:
2. I've got a passport.
3. I haven't got a lot of money.
4. My friend has got a lot of problems.
5. We haven't got a fast computer.

C.

2. Has; hasn't
3. have; don't
4. got; 's (has)
5. Does; doesn't
6. got; haven't

Exercise 10

3. plays
4. sings
5. 's studying (is studying) *or* studies
6. loves
7. seems
8. sings
9. doesn't understand (does not understand)
10. is learning
11. needs
12. forgets
13. has
14. go *or* are going
15. likes
16. do
17. eat
18. go
19. aren't thinking (are not thinking)
20. is studying
21. doesn't do (does not do)
22. speaks
23. 's helping (is helping)
24. are making

Exercise 11

Answers will vary.
Sample answers:
1. I don't remember my first day of school because I was only three.
2. I listen to music on my way to school every day.
3. We're not doing this exercise on the computer.
4. My brother plays the guitar well.
5. I don't understand English grammar.
6. It's not raining hard right now.
7. My father doesn't use a computer at work very often.
8. It doesn't rain a lot here in the summer.
9. My parents don't like lazy people.
10. I send e-mail to some of my friends every day.
11. I've got exciting plans for tonight: I'm going to the concert.
12. I'm not watching TV now.

Exercise 12

A.

2. b. played tennis with a friend.
3. a. were tired Friday night
   b. didn't go (did not go) to the gym
4. a. brought her lunch to work yesterday
   b. She didn't eat (did not eat) in a restaurant with her friends.
5. a. was late for work this morning
   b. He didn't get up (did not get up) at 7:30.
6. a. didn't drive (did not drive) to Miami last week
   b. They flew first class.

B.
2. did Steve do his homework
3. were Andrew and Megan tired last night
4. Where did Jessica's friends eat?
5. Why did Martin get up late this morning?
6. When did Nicolas and Rosa fly to Miami?

Exercise 13
2. moved
3. drove
4. were
5. wanted
6. read
7. learned
8. were
9. brought
10. was
11. arrived
12. took
13. passed
14. was
15. made
16. was

Exercise 14
2. *A:* Were you sleeping
   B: I was dreaming
3. *B:* What was I doing?
   A: You were driving
   B: I was coming; I was concentrating
4. *A:* was Sue crying
   B: She wasn't crying (was not crying);
   She was laughing; Some friends were telling
5. *A:* you were talking
   B: I was living; She and my wife were working

Exercise 15
2. *A:* Did you go out last night?
   B: was raining; didn't want (did not want) to get wet
3. *A:* missed; was leaving; arrived
   B: finished; was sitting
4. *A:* called; answered
   B: was watching; didn't hear (did not hear)
5. *A:* did Tim hurt himself
   B: was playing soccer in the park; fell
6. *A:* did you do; happened
   B: called the police
7. *A:* were you doing; went out
   B: was cooking dinner
8. *A:* Did you see John at work today?
   B: didn't have (did not have) time to talk

Exercise 16
2. go to bed early; used to stay up late
3. owns a restaurant; he used to be a professional baseball player
4. go out a lot; but they used to stay home every night
5. is bald now, but he used to have long hair
6. drives a car now, but she used to ride a bike
7. eats at home now, but he used to eat in restaurants
8. is a very big city now, but it used to be a small place

Exercise 17
2. was
3. broke
4. Was anyone else
5. didn't go (did not go)
6. saw
7. was sleeping
8. did you come
9. Did you see
10. was
11. was sitting
12. didn't think (did not think)
13. Did anyone see
14. were preparing
15. were watching
16. Did the thieves take
17. didn't know (did not know)
18. were looking
19. chose
20. were taking
21. got
22. called

Exercise 18
Answers will vary.
Sample answers:
1. I wasn't eating dinner at 7 P.M. last night; I ate at 8.
2. I didn't use to go to bed early when I was a child.
3. I was sleeping at 2:30 in the morning.
4. I didn't drive to work last week because I was on vacation.
5. I went to the movies yesterday.
6. I used to play soccer when I was a child.
7. I didn't stay at home last night.
8. I used to study a lot when I was in secondary school.
9. My sister had an accident when she was driving home the other night.
10. My roommate was talking on the phone at six this morning.
11. My mother cried when she heard the bad news.

Exercise 19

A.

Answers will vary.
Sample answers:
2. I've never sung (I have never sung) in public.
3. I've never driven (I have never driven) a truck.
4. I've eaten (I have eaten) alone in a restaurant many times.
5. I've changed (I have changed) a flat tire once.
6. I've never cooked (I have never cooked) dinner for ten people.
7. I've been (I have been) to Paris twice.
8. I've never broken (I have never broken) an arm.

B.

2. sung in public
3. Have you ever driven a truck?
4. Have you ever eaten alone in a restaurant?
5. Have you ever changed a flat tire?
6. Have you ever cooked dinner for ten people?
7. Have you ever been to Paris?
8. Have you ever broken an arm?

Exercise 20

3. has he been waiting for
4. How long has she been
5. How long have they been traveling?
6. How long have you been studying
7. How long have you had
8. How long have they lived

Exercise 21

4. had it a half hour ago
5. 's been raining (has been raining) for a long time
6. moved to Boston six months ago
7. he's been (he has been) there for almost three weeks
8. I've had (have had) dark hair since I was little
9. I took some aspirin an hour ago
10. they've been living (they have been living) *or* they've lived (they have lived) there since 1982
11. he's been studying (he has been studying) medicine for three years
12. we've known (we have known) each other since we were in high school

Exercise 22

A.

3. 've already been (have already been) there
4. I've already read (have already read) it
5. Have you seen the boss yet?
6. haven't gotten (have not gotten) it yet
7. Have you gone to the post office yet?

B.

2. just got up
3. already spoke to her
4. didn't tell (did not tell) him yet

Exercise 23

3. My friends have never eaten Ethiopian food.
4. What time did you wake up this morning?
5. My friend has had the same job since college.
6. Have you ever been to Norway?
7. Did you eat a lot of good food on your last vacation?
8. I didn't meet (did not meet) your parents until two years ago.
9. Did you lose your wallet at home or at work?
10. Dean's father started his new job last week.
11. Have you ever stayed at a hotel on the beach?
12. Janeen has known her best friend since elementary school.

Exercise 24

Answers will vary.
Sample answers:
1. I've lived in this town all my life.
2. I've known my best friend since I was five.
3. I've had the same hair style for two years.
4. I bought something expensive two days ago.
5. I've never seen an elephant before.
6. I've never been to Australia.
7. My life has changed a lot since my marriage.
8. I haven't done my homework yet.
9. I took a long vacation last year.
10. I was sick for a few days last week.
11. My father has worked at the same office for a long time.
12. I just remembered the name of the new movie.
13. I went to bed early last night.
14. My cousins have lived in many places around the world.
15. I've already eaten lunch.

Exercise 25

3. They were sent to my old address.
3. It is found in only a few places.
4. It wasn't played (was not played) much twenty years ago.
6. Oil is not imported by Venezuela.
7. Was anything stolen?
8. *A:* Was anyone injured in the accident?
   B: Two people were taken to the hospital.
9. How many people are needed to make a basketball team?
10. They are called "daffodils."
11. When was this package delivered here?

Exercise 26

2. b
3. c
4. a
5. b
6. b
7. c
8. a
9. b

Exercise 27

4. was invented
5. are sent
6. are checked
7. was broken
8. 's being built (is being built)
9. it's being used (it is being used)
10. they're sold (they are sold)
11. they were cut down
12. 's been cleaned (has been cleaned)
13. 'm being helped (am being helped)
14. they're being taken care of (They are being taken care of)

Exercise 28

Answers will vary.
Sample answers:
1. The office building was built in less than two years.
2. Several languages are spoken in Switzerland.
3. A good program about ancient Egypt was recently shown on TV.
4. My favorite pasta dish is made with many ingredients, including peas.
5. My computer has been repaired; it runs well.
6. My sister is invited to a lot of parties.
7. Many buildings were destroyed in the big earthquake in San Francisco.
8. Only classical music is played on this radio station.
9. Some children are named for their parents.
10. A new drug for arthritis was developed recently.

Exercise 29

2. *A:* Is
   B: was
3. *A:* doesn't (does not)
   B: does
   A: didn't (did not)
4. *A:* 've (have); Have
   B: Did
   A: 've (have)
   B: Did
5. *A:* Was
   B: didn't (did not); 's (is)

6. *A:* Did
   B: haven't (have not); Did
   A: didn't (did not)
   B: did
7. *A:* Have
   B: 'm (am)
   B: Are

Exercise 30

A.

2. have
3. was
4. Do
5. Does
6. Have
7. Are
8. Did
9. Is

B.

2. got
3. came
4. used
5. understood
6. took
7. broke
8. found
9. used

Exercise 31

3. 's discussing (is discussing) her company's new products in the afternoon
4. She isn't staying (is not staying) with relatives in Denver.
5. Tuesday she's having (is having) lunch with a college friend.
6. In the evening she's going out (she is going out) with her in-laws.
7. They're seeing (they are seeing) a play.
8. The play begins at 8.
9. Her flight on Wednesday leaves very early.
10. She's returning (She is returning) to Atlanta on Wednesday.
11. Her husband isn't meeting (is not meeting) her at the airport.
12. Her bus departs from the airport at 11 A.M.
13. She's not going (She is not going) to the office on Wednesday.

Exercise 32

2. a. going to study Native Americans in April
   b. 'll bring (will bring) pictures of our family trip to Arizona
3. a. We're going to plant (We are going to plant) a garden in the school yard in the spring.
   b. We'll bring (We will bring) some seeds from home.

4. a. We're going to have (We are going to have) a party next month.
   b. My mother will make cookies for us.

Exercise 33

Answers will vary.
Sample answers:
1. I'm going to buy a new car next year. I think I'll have enough money by then.
2. I'm not going to take a trip to Hawaii next winter. I don't think I'll take a vacation in the winter.
3. I'm going to change jobs soon. I think I'll look for a job closer to home.
4. I'm going to take an aerobics class next month. I think I'll take it at the local community center on Saturday morning.
5. I'm not going to visit relatives in the next two or three months. I think I'll visit my cousins in Florida next winter.
6. I'm going to get some new clothes soon. I think I'll go shopping when there are the big sales.
7. I'm not going to spend a lot of money this coming year. I don't think I'll do any traveling next year.
8. I'm going to move to another city in a few months. I don't think I'll move until May.

Exercise 34

3. be in town next week
4. might rain tomorrow
5. The driver might not know the way to our house.
6. Manuel might forget to call us.
7. We might go to Central America for vacation.
8. My friends might do volunteer work this weekend.
9. You might have a cold.
10. James might not be on time for work tomorrow.
11. I might watch TV tonight.
12. We might not recognize Uncle Joe when we see him.

Exercise 35

4. Could *or* Can; use
5. can't find
6. Could *or* Can; get
7. couldn't decide
8. can speak
9. could; read
10. can play
11. couldn't sleep

Exercise 36

3. must not like rice
4. must not know it very well
5. must not drink coffee
6. must be vegetarians
7. must know him
8. must have children

9. must be upset
10. must not feel well today

Exercise 37

2. should go to work today
3. I don't think she should use her phone while she is driving.
4. I don't think he should make noise near a hospital.
5. I think she should drive more carefully.
6. I don't think they should watch TV for such a long time.
7. I don't think they should go for a walk right now.
8. I think she should ask for help to fix her flat tire.

Exercise 38

A.

4. Do drivers have to have insurance in this state?
5. Tourists don't have to have a local driver's license in many places.
6. Drivers have to wear seat belts.

B.

3. must take a shower before going into the pool
4. must not park your car in front of the fire station
5. must not smoke in this building

Exercise 39

2. *A:* Do you like your Spanish class?
3. *A:* 'd like to buy (would like to buy) Gary a present.
   A: likes music a lot
4. *A:* What would you like to drink?
   A: Would you like sugar in it? *or* Do you like sugar in it?
5. *A:* Do you like foreign movies?
   A: Would you like to go tonight?

Exercise 40

2. *A:* Where would you like to sit?
3. *B:* 'd rather not tell (I would rather not tell) her
4. *A:* What would you like to have for dessert?
5. *B:* 'd rather be (would rather be) a teacher
6. *B:* 'd rather not move (would rather not move) there
7. *B:* wouldn't like to be (would not like to be) in his position
8. *B:* 'd rather go (would rather go) to a small college than a large one.
9. *B:* 'd rather go out (would rather go out) than eat at home.

Exercise 41

3. Pay the bills next week. *or* Pay them next week.
   Don't pay (Do not pay) the bills this week. *or*
   Don't pay them this week.
4. Wear a suit and tie.
   Don't wear (Do not wear) your old tennis shoes.
5. Let's invite my relatives.
   Let's not invite your relatives.
6. Get some fruit and yogurt.
   Don't get (Do not get) any cookies this time.
7. Let's go to a new restaurant.
   Let's not go to the same old place.
8. Let's go to Montreal this time.
   Let's not go to Alaska again.

Exercise 42

4. can help us move on Saturday
5. She's going to watch (She is going to watch) the
   game on TV Sunday.
6. She might plant a garden next spring.
7. She's not going to be (She is not going to be)/She
   isn't going to be (is not going to be) at home
   tomorrow night.
8. She can't play (cannot play) chess this afternoon.
9. She might go to Colombia next summer.
10. She can't go (cannot go) shopping with us
    on Thursday.

Exercise 43

3. must like
4. might fall
5. would like to eat
6. have to turn off *or* must turn off; must not use *or*
   can't (cannot) use
7. should not talk *or* must not talk
8. must be
9. must be; can't (cannot) stay awake
10. can't (cannot) see the movie; should move
11. must not agree *or* might not agree; would rather sit
12. must have *or* might have
13. must not be

Exercise 44

Answers will vary.
Sample answers:
1. use computers
2. (couldn't) stay up late on school nights
3. shop for my grandmother
4. shop for my grandmother
5. talk to their children about goals, concerns, and
   problems
6. take small children to restaurants
7. to lose their jobs because of layoffs
8. watch the basketball game; the soccer game
9. not be very careful
10. find ways to get food to poor people

11. to work in a restaurant; work in a store
12. sing; try out for the choir
13. check over their writing
14. takes a big piece of cake; get any
15. go to a doctor

Exercise 45

3. There is a mailbox on this street.
4. There are two cats in the window.
5. There is a flower garden in the front yard.
6. There is grass in the yard.
7. There is one tree in the yard.
8. There isn't (is not) a truck in front of the house.
9. There is a garage behind the house.
10. There are police in the neighborhood now.
11. There are three birds on the chimney.
12. There are three chairs in the yard.
13. There is one bike against the house.
14. There isn't (is not) a child in the yard.

Exercise 46

3. There is
4. There have been
5. There will be
6. there was
7. There were
8. There is/are
9. There has been
10. There is
11. There will be
12. There is
13. There were

Exercise 47

4. It's (It is) windy.
5. It's (It is) almost 500 miles
6. it was dark and cold
7. there was a big conference there last year
8. there was a lot of traffic on the highway
9. it isn't (is not) hot enough
10. there was a train at 9:30
11. It was difficult to find a parking space.
12. there weren't (were not) many people in the
    ticket line

Exercise 48

A.

Answers will vary.
Sample answers:
3. Yes, I do. *or* No, I don't.
4. Yes, I will. *or* No, I won't.
5. Yes, I was. *or* No, I wasn't.
6. Yes, I did. *or* No, I didn't.
7. Yes, I am. *or* No, I'm not.
8. Yes, it was. *or* No, it wasn't.

9. Yes, there are. *or* No, there aren't.
10. Yes, I have. *or* No, I haven't.

B.

3. hasn't (has not)
4. don't (do not)
5. did
6. doesn't (does not)
7. 'm not (am not)
8. won't (will not)
9. have
10. might

Exercise 49

4. You did? So did I.
5. You're not? Neither am I.
6. You can't? Neither can I.
7. You will? So will I.
8. You're not? Neither am I.
9. You don't? Neither do I.
10. You have? So have I.
11. You would? So would I.
12. He couldn't? Neither could I.
13. They don't? Neither do I.
14. He is? So am I.

Exercise 50

3. do you; b
4. won't you; j
5. are there; l
6. have you; k
7. didn't she; a
8. are you; c
9. do you; i
10. aren't you; g
11. weren't you; h
12. are they; e

Exercise 51

3. I don't go (do not go) to bed early when I'm not sleepy.
4. Fish don't have (do not have) wings, but birds do.
5. Don't read (Do not read) that book if you don't find it interesting.
6. You shouldn't work (should not work) extra hours if you don't feel well.
7. I walked to school because the buses weren't running (were not running) because of bad weather.
8. We didn't eat (did not eat) the fish because it didn't smell very good to us.
9. They don't study (do not study) very hard, so they don't get very good grades.
10. Sheila wasn't (was not) here yesterday, so she didn't hear the news.
11. I won't see you tomorrow if you can't be here.

Exercise 52

3. My boss hasn't been (has not been) to Canada
4. My brother can fix a car
5. The Mendozas aren't (are not) from Mexico
6. My car isn't (is not) for sale
7. I caught the flu last year
8. I didn't watch (did not watch) the news last night
9. My father doesn't like (does not like) his job
10. Tony isn't doing (is not doing) his homework now
11. Edgar was born in Canada
12. I won't be (will not be) at work tomorrow
13. I should work a little harder
14. I wouldn't like (would not like) to live in a big city

Exercise 53

Answers will vary.
Sample answers:
1. My wife doesn't speak French
2. and so did my cousin
3. I like to play soccer
4. My teacher is from Russia
5. My friend didn't pass the driving test
6. and neither do I
7. My friends have decided on careers
8. I don't have an extra pen
9. but no one in my family does.
10. My cousin will finish school in January
11. I haven't been to the new sports stadium
12. Most students haven't been able to do the homework
13. My sister hasn't washed the dishes
14. and neither do I
15. My friend would jump from a parachute
16. but I am
17. My friend studied English as a child

Exercise 54

2. would you like to visit
3. have you bought [for the trip]
4. does your plane leave
5. does it take to fly to Hawaii
6. did the tickets cost
7. haven't you told your parents [about the trip]
8. trips do you take [every year]
9. did you go to Puerto Rico
10. did you travel [a few months ago]
11. were you planning to go
12. did you change your mind [about going there]
13. have you been there
14. do you go there
15. vacation time do you have

Exercise 55

3. did you see
4. is happening
5. happened to you yesterday

6. lives in a castle
7. do your neighbors have *or* do they have
8. woke you up this morning
9. do you eat for breakfast every morning
10. do you know
11. teaches physics
12. did you ask for directions
13. fixed the broken window
14. do we need [for the recipe]
15. surprised you yesterday

Exercise 56

A.

2. are you waiting for
3. do they belong to
4. are you writing to
5. did you lend it to
6. hotel did you stay at
7. was it about
8. are you traveling with

B.

3. What was the traffic like?
4. What are/were they like?
5. What were they like?

Exercise 57

3. What time
4. How tall
5. How big
6. What kind
7. How far
8. Which
9. What kind
10. How often
11. How much
12. Which
13. How tall
14. Who
15. How long

Exercise 58

3. size is this sweater
4. How much did you spend on the present?
5. Which shirt do you like?
6. How long have you been working here?
7. What kind of music do you like?
8. How often do you go to church?
9. What color are her eyes?
10. Which coat is yours?
11. How long does it take to learn a language?
12. How much were the flowers?
13. How long will it take you to drive to the beach?
14. What kind of flowers should we buy?
15. How long did it take you to paint your house?

Exercise 59

Answers will vary.
Sample answers:
4. I'm not sure what "silly" means.
5. I think I know who Abraham Lincoln was.
6. I don't know how a computer works.
7. I think I know who John F. Kennedy married.
8. I don't know how many times astronauts have gone to the moon.
9. I'm not sure when Mother Teresa was born.
10. I'm not sure how long it takes to fly from Beijing to New York City.
11. I don't know how much a house in Moscow costs.
12. I don't know how many calories there are in an apple.
13. No one knows why people make war.
14. No one knows how many people have died in wars.
15. I'm not sure if/whether it rained more a hundred years ago.

Exercise 60

Answers will vary.
Sample answers:
1. do the Westons live
2. does Mr. Weston do
3. did the Westons move to the neighborhood
4. did the Westons move
5. Mrs. Weston a teacher
6. the Westons have a pet
7. house the Westons live in
8. car Mr. Weston drives
9. you visit the Westons yet
10. you met the Westons yet
11. Mr. Weston doesn't work downtown
12. The Weston children went to school this week
13. Mr. Weston to get to work

Exercise 61

2. she was a vegetarian
3. Larry said; he was very sick today
4. Matt told; he had to visit his aunt in the hospital
5. Alex and Susan said; they were going to get up early on Saturday
6. Mrs. Holden told; her son could play the violin beautifully
7. Bill's aunt said; she had just sent him some money for his birthday
8. told; he wouldn't tell (would not tell) anyone my secret
9. Aunt Claudia said; she didn't eat (did not eat) sweets

Exercise 62

3. study harder
4. sleep; last night
5. go with *or* come with; watching his little brother
6. having *or* eating
7. be
8. to go shopping; have any money
9. talk to Gloria; taking
10. to work for his brother
11. to wait

Exercise 63

3. to visit Egypt one day
4. giving me a ride to the doctor's tomorrow afternoon
5. to give me a ride home; to walk *or* walking
6. leaving at 7 tomorrow morning; to leave at 7:30 *or* to leave later
7. to go to the movies; writing her report [for work]
8. cleaning her room
9. to go to the mountains this weekend
10. to be; to be a teacher

Exercise 64

2. her son to pick up his dirty clothes; to pick
3. going to the beach; being out in the sun on weekends
4. Jennie to buy; to buy
5. Jason wait
6. Bert to work on Saturday; working

Exercise 65

2. ask the teacher about the test
3. a wedding
4. relax and meet new people
5. to help me with my Arabic
6. for the babysitter to
7. buy a present
8. me to finish
9. learn how to use a computer
10. a conference
11. you to answer *or* your answer to

Exercise 66

Answers will vary.
Sample answers:
1. walking along the river
2. to have a lot of money
3. to play the piano
4. swim; I never took lessons
5. go to the concert; have enough money
6. watching comedies on TV
7. to call my mother
8. speak English; to speak as much as you can
9. washing dishes; doing laundry

10. to clean the garage; to break anything
11. my friend to go to the museum with me; him to go
12. where I'm studying English
13. to get a good job with a big company
14. to answer the question; it was too personal
15. learn how to cook; like eating out all the time
16. to take a vacation; cost a lot of money

Exercise 67

Answers will vary.
Sample answers:
1. sending e-mail; talking on the phone
2. typing my report on a computer; to play loud music
3. to go to the gym every day; go there
4. go with you to the beach; going to visit my cousins
5. eating/to eat good food; cooking
6. the children watch TV after school; the children to do their homework first
7. me to take the medicine every day; to take it
8. my friend to help me fix my car; to fix on my own
9. spending more time in the computer lab; find the time
10. plant a garden last year; want to plant one this year
11. to go to see the fireworks in the park; to stay home and watch TV
12. get some exercise today; stay home
13. stay longer; to get home after dark
14. me to go to the meeting; me work late
15. to the store; a newspaper

Exercise 68

3. went to Poland on vacation
4. 're going (are going) skiing *or* 're going (are going) to go skiing
5. go for a walk
6. going on a business trip
7. gone shopping
8. going to work *or* are going to go to work
9. going to a movie *or* going to go to a movie
10. going to the drugstore for some aspirin *or* going to go to . . .
11. went on strike

Exercise 69

2. got married
3. getting tired
4. got on the bus; got off the bus
5. got out of the taxi
6. getting wet
7. get her
8. get home
9. *A:* get here; got lost
   B: getting ready
10. get there
11. get to work
12. got into the car

Exercise 70

2. doing
3. do
4. make
5. make
6. do
7. do
8. did
9. doing
10. doing
11. making
12. doing
13. done
14. do
15. make
16. do

Exercise 71

3. How many accidents did you have?
4. Do you have your key? *or* Have you got your key?
5. Did you have a bad flight?
6. Has your sister had her baby yet? *or* Did your sister have her baby yet?
7. Did you have an argument with your brother?
8. Did you have the flu last week?
9. Did you have a good time at the concert?

Exercise 72

2. *A:* do
   B: makes; do
   A: have
   B: did; got
3. *A:* making
   B: having; get
   A: do; make
   B: get
4. *A:* get; getting
   B: have *or* get
5. *A:* make
   A: make
6. *A:* have
   B: had; do; do; make

Exercise 73

Answers will vary.
Sample answers:
1. I never do housework during the week, only on the weekends.
2. I always go to bed late on Friday night.
3. My father always gets to work a half hour early.
4. My brother is going to get married soon.
5. My sister had a baby not long ago.
6. I like to go shopping at the mall at lunchtime.
7. My neighbor had a car accident a while ago, and he was badly hurt.
8. I made a terrible mistake when I moved from my old apartment.
9. I always have a big party on my birthday.
10. I'm going to get ready after I finish doing the dishes.
11. I never do exercises at night; I always exercise in the morning.
12. My mother always makes a list before she goes grocery shopping.

Exercise 74

3. I like them
4. Do you like them?
5. Do they like them?
6. I don't like (do not like) it
7. it doesn't like (does not like) us
8. He likes it
9. She doesn't like (does not like) it
10. like them
11. He doesn't like (does not like) it
12. She likes it
13. I like them
14. They don't like (do not like) it

Exercise 75

3. it; them
4. it; me
5. them; it
6. them; us
7. it; me
8. her; them/me
9. it; you
10. them; her
11. it; them
12. them; me
13. it; him
14. it; me
15. them; her
16. it; me
17. them; him
18. them; her *or* her; them

Exercise 76

2. a
3. c
4. a
5. b
6. c

Exercise 77

4. it
5. her
6. it
7. me
8. his
9. her

10. hers
11. him
12. them
13. their
14. mine
15. theirs
16. them
17. my
18. yours
19. mine

Exercise 78

2. Two women are sitting on the same bench and talking to each other.
3. The girl on the swing is enjoying herself.
4. The young man and young woman on rollerblades are waving at each other.
5. The child is saying, "I want to feed the pigeons by myself."
6. A girl with two dogs is angry at them. The dogs are enjoying themselves, however.
7. The boy with the skateboard hurt himself when he fell.
8. The woman is telling her two friends, "Enjoy yourselves at the park."

Exercise 79

3. My father's job
4. Susan's party
5. My uncles' wives
6. The bottom of your package
7. your brother's little girl and boy
8. the color of your hair
9. children's names
10. My son's in-laws
11. The condition of your teeth
12. Kathy's doctor

Exercise 80

Answers will vary.
Sample answers:
1. His car isn't reliable, and my car is new, so we usually use mine to go places together.
2. My friend's mother is looking for him.
3. The beginning of the story was exciting.
4. My parents' apartment is near mine, and I often visit them.
5. We hurt ourselves when we tried to move the heavy furniture.
6. My friends couldn't fix the electricity by themselves, so they asked him for help.
7. Don't study for the test by yourselves; study with each other.
8. My friends got angry with each other when they were doing the school project.

9. My computer is old and slow, but hers is new and fast.
10. My neighbors and I have cats. Theirs is a Siamese and mine is a Persian.
11. I think that he painted the house by himself.
12. The telephone number of that company is in the phone book.
13. They have a ladder, and they told us we could use it.

Exercise 81

3. This is an American restaurant.
4. There are two children in the family.
5. The mother is wearing pants.
6. The boys are wearing shorts and shirts.
7. There are flowers on each table.
8. There are shelves on the back wall of the restaurant.
9. There are dishes on the top shelf.
10. There are knives, forks, and spoons on the middle shelf.
11. There's (There is) a bowl with an apple on the bottom shelf.
12. There's (There is) a mouse under one of the tables.
13. The restaurant is open for three hours at lunchtime.
14. A woman is ordering food.
15. There are fish in the fish tank.

Exercise 82

2. a. glue, a place to work, a ruler, tools, wood
   b. a computer, a university class
3. a. a guitar, lessons, a person to listen or people to listen, a piece of music or pieces of music, a teacher, time to practice
   b. a dentist, long hair, an orchestra, a piano, a test
4. a. a blanket or blankets, a carpet or carpets, dishes, forks, furniture, money, pillows, pots and pans, a refrigerator, a stove, towels
   b. a car, a diamond or diamonds, vegetables
5. a. a garden, seeds, a shovel, soil, water
   b. an engineer, a hammer, a knife, scissors
6. a. a dictionary, an idea, information, paper, time to think
   b. a new hat, a TV program

Exercise 83

2. a piece of chicken; some rice
3. Some bread; cans of beans
4. long brown hair, a small nose; eyes
5. some warm clothing; new suitcases
6. a bottle of perfume; some earrings
7. A: some apples
   B: some ice cream
8. A: glasses of water
   B: some lemonade

Exercise 84

2. X
3. X
4. a
5. The
6. X
7. the
8. X
9. X
10. the
11. the
12. the
13. X
14. the
15. the
16. the
17. a
18. a
19. X
20. X
21. X
22. X
23. X
24. a
25. X
26. X
27. a
28. X
29. X
30. a
31. the
32. the
33. X

Exercise 85

Answers will vary.
Sample answers:
2. Grand Canyon National Park is bigger than the London Zoo.
3. Indonesia has more people than the United Arab Emirates.
4. The Vatican Museums have more old things than the Museum of Science and Industry in Chicago.
5. The Himalayas are higher than the Alps.
6. Asia has a larger population than Western Europe.
7. Japan has more land than the Philippines.
8. The Empire State Building is taller than the Washington Monument.
9. The Colosseum is older than the Great Wall of China.
10. Wall Street is more famous than Columbus Avenue.
11. In the Northern Hemisphere, more cold winds come from the north.

Exercise 86

Answers will vary.
Sample answers:
1. We had a big English test last month, and we're going to have another big text next week.
2. I usually listen to the news on the radio, not on TV.
3. There were an apple and an orange in the bowl, and I ate the orange.
4. An engineer came and fixed the boiler within an hour.
5. I ate a salad and some pizza for lunch.
6. There was a book on the floor under the couch, but it wasn't the book I wanted.
7. We asked at the hotel where we could rent a car.
8. My cousin goes to work at 4 and returns home at midnight.
9. True friends are the friends who help you when you are in trouble.
10. Information about the accident was on the front page of the newspaper.
11. My friend wrote a letter to the newspaper to ask for advice about a personal problem.

Exercise 87

A.

2. g
3. e
4. h
5. j
6. d
7. a
8. i
9. b
10. f

B.

3. Are these your pencils?; they are
4. Is this your lunch?; it isn't
5. Is this your book?; it isn't
6. Are these your pictures?; they are
7. are
8. isn't
9. Are those your scissors?; they are
10. Is that your apple?; it is
11. Is that your bottle of water?; it isn't
12. Are those your soccer shoes?; they aren't

Exercise 88

3. Look for nice, fresh ones. *or* Look for some nice, fresh ones.
4. don't need (do not need) any
5. Do you have smaller ones? *or* Do you have any smaller ones?
6. eats in expensive ones
7. one did you stay

8. A: Do we need any rice?
   B: have some
9. 're looking (are looking) for a small one with four doors
10. doesn't have (does not have) any friends

Exercise 89

A.

2. There are no new people on the list.
3. This store has no fresh tomatoes.
4. There is no reason for you to stay home tonight.
5. Mr. Ryan has no patience with his children.
6. I had no problems with your car.
7. There's (There is) no milk in the refrigerator.
8. There are no clouds in the sky today.

B.

4. Nothing. They didn't say (did not say) anything about you.
5. Nothing. I'm not (I am not) angry about anything.
6. No one. or Nobody. I'm not (I am not) angry at anyone.
7. None. I didn't spend (did not spend) any money.
8. Nothing. I'm not listening (I am not listening) to anything.

Exercise 90

1. something
2. A: somebody / someone
   B: nobody / no one; somebody / someone
3. A: something
   B: anything
   A: anything
   B: Nobody / No one
4. A: anywhere
   B: something
5. A: anything
   B: anything; anybody / anyone
6. A: anywhere; somewhere
   B: somebody / someone; anything

Exercise 91

2. All people need food.
3. There aren't (are not) any fresh flowers for sale today.
4. All of the secretaries were on time this morning. or All the secretaries . . . .
5. Some people don't like (do not like) to live in the country.
6. Most of my friends have driver's licenses.
7. Not every student in my class studies hard.
8. None of my cousins live/lives in this state.
9. Every driver has to have insurance in this state.
10. Everybody in my office is married.

Exercise 92

3. None of it is left.
4. Most of it was eaten.
5. None of them were drunk.
6. Most of it was drunk.
7. Some of it was eaten.
8. All of them were used.
9. Most of it was eaten.

Exercise 93

2. of them are married or of the boys . . .
3. neither of them is married or neither of the girls . . .
4. both of them have children or both of the boys . . .
5. All of them live in Chicago. or All of the children . . .
6. none of them live / lives with their parents or none of the children . . .
7. Amy doesn't live (does not live) with either of them. or . . . either of her brothers.
8. Both of; have jobs; neither of
9. None of them is a lawyer. or None of the children is a lawyer. or None of them are lawyers. or None of the children are lawyers.
10. Neither of them is a teacher. or Neither of the sisters . . .
11. most of them are in school or most of the children . . .
12. all of them know how to cook or all of the children . . .
13. Both of the girls; neither of the boys

Exercise 94

A.

3. She goes to the movies a lot.
4. He gives a lot of love to his children.
5. She doesn't have (does not have) much free time. or . . . a lot of free time.
6. He has many problems. or . . . a lot of problems.
7. They don't eat (do not eat) at home much or . . . a lot.
8. He has many friends. or . . . a lot of friends.

B.

3. very little
4. a little
5. a few
6. very few
7. very little
8. very few

Exercise 95

2. a lot of
3. much
4. little
5. many
6. few

7. a lot of
8. a lot of
9. a few
10. many
11. a little
12. a lot of

Exercise 96

2. That
3. those
4. anybody *or* anyone
5. anybody *or* anyone
6. nobody *or* no one
7. anything
8. somewhere
9. something
10. anybody *or* anyone
11. no
12. ones
13. any
14. None
15. That

Exercise 97

Answers will vary.
Sample answers:
1. want friends
2. have gone to college
3. work very long hours
4. I gave some of the cookies I made to my friends at work
5. let their children play video games or watch TV for long hours
6. relatives live/lives near here
7. are going to go downtown for the free rock concert
8. I visited both my grandfathers in Poland last year
9. are very good at being friendly to strangers
10. have two cars in their garages
11. I found two lamps at the garage sale
12. "Which of the two hair dryers is working?" asked my sister.
13. is going to come to our party

Exercise 98

3. strange
4. careful; the used car
5. well but slowly
6. My brother; well
7. The judge; clear and brief; my question
8. The mail always; late on Saturday
9. quiet but good
10. reckless
11. heavily

Exercise 99

3. Mexico City is bigger than Lima.
4. The Nile River is longer than the Amazon.
5. Tokyo is more crowded than Nairobi.
6. New York is closer to Montreal than to Miami.
7. Iceland is farther north than England.
8. Hawaii has nicer weather than Alaska.
9. Puerto Rico has worse rainstorms than Egypt.
10. Moscow has colder winters than London.
11. Australia is larger than New Zealand.
12. The Petronas Towers in Malaysia are taller than the Sears Tower in Chicago.

Exercise 100

2. as big as Canada
3. lived here as long as
4. get up as early as your mother
5. as expensive as cherries
6. as popular as soccer
7. you work as hard as your father
8. Is a cold as bad as the flu?
9. Does your sister go out as much as your brother [does]?
10. Do dentists have as many patients as doctors [do]?

Exercise 101

3. as
4. same
5. more
6. as
7. as
8. much
9. less
10. less
11. little

Exercise 102

Answers will vary.
Sample answers:
4. The bird is the noisiest.
5. The cat is most interesting to watch.
6. The cat is the nicest pet.
7. The fish is the easiest to feed.
8. The cat is the most popular pet.
9. The cat is the most pleasant to hold.
10 The cat is the most dangerous for children.
11. The bird is the prettiest.
12. The fish is hardest to take along on vacation.
13. The cat is the most difficult to take care of.
14. The fish is the best birthday present for a child.

Exercise 103

4. 'm (am) strong enough to move
5. warm enough to go swimming
6. get enough practice

7. enough clean plates for everyone
8. big enough for me
9. hard enough
10. enough gas to get
11. enough time to finish
12. the soup salty enough for you

Exercise 104

A.

4. 's (is) too hot to play
5. were too small for me
6. talks too much
7. was too busy to see me
8. was too much snow
9. were too many people
10. costs too much

B.

3. too young to get married
4. too much coffee
5. 's (is) too little to play soccer
6. enough money for your trip
7. too many mistakes
8. don't get (do not get) enough sleep

Exercise 105

Answers will vary.
Sample answers:

1. It is good to drive slowly under bad weather conditions even if other drivers get angry.
2. If you are nervous, you'll probably do badly on the test.
3. The desk clerk at the hotel sounded foreign.
4. My brother is usually slow getting ready in the morning, but today he was late and got ready quickly.
5. Bread tastes delicious when it is eaten hot from the oven.
6. My friend looked surprised when I gave her a birthday gift.
7. My house is quiet early in the morning, and I can work well at that time.
8. People should drive carefully around the dangerous curve.
9. After I worked in the garden for a couple hours, I suddenly felt tired.
10. I think that most people look good in blue.
11. When people speak very softly, it is difficult to understand them.

Exercise 106

3. the most interesting job
4. Mrs. Reese is busier
5. The Grill is the most expensive restaurant.
6. as good as Mike's
7. longer than

8. as high as Everest
9. Mrs. Johnson is the most patient
10. Jupiter is larger than
11. storm was the worst [one] *or* was the worst storm
12. the cheapest TV
13. the most expensive shoes

Exercise 107

4. as crowded
5. more often
6. more expensive
7. as nice
8. prettiest
9. as many
10. closest
11. more difficult
12. more interesting
13. best
14. warmer
15. sunnier
16. nicest

Exercise 108

2. My sister doesn't like my new car very much.
3. Mark and Amy both work in the same office.
4. Samantha met him at a party last month.
5. The Wymans still go dancing at a club every weekend.
6. Do you ever leave dirty dishes in the kitchen overnight?
7. Have you already met my boss?
8. Clare seldom has time to go out with her friends on weekends.
9. I still have to buy some stamps at the post office this afternoon.
10. Do you sometimes forget to turn off the lights at night?
11. Fred doesn't usually eat dinner at home after work.
12. My two uncles are both police officers.

Exercise 109

3. still play
4. already have
5. come yet
6. *A:* found; yet
   B: still looking
7. told; yet
8. already seen
9. aren't (are not) *or* haven't gotten; yet
10. already washed *or* already done
11. still working

Exercise 110

A.

3. it to them
4. them to her
5. them for you
6. it for us
7. it to me
8. it to them

B.

2. me a picture of their baby
3. my neighbor a cup of sugar
4. their parents a car
5. my father a newspaper

Exercise 111

Answers will vary.
Sample answers:

1. I have never forgotten my mother's birthday.
2. My sister bought a dog, and she gave it to me on my birthday.
3. The students are usually in the classroom before class begins.
4. I was late for class yesterday, and Betty was also late.
5. Are you still wearing those old jeans?
6. I never lend anything to strangers.
7. They showed us the photos from their trip to the Grand Canyon.
8. My family rarely goes out to eat.
9. I haven't been to the new mall yet.
10. I have already learned the news about the accident.
11. Many people eat breakfast in a restaurant on the weekend.

Exercise 112

A.

2. X; X; in
3. at; in
4. X; X
5. X; in; at

B.

3. I have a coffee break at 4 P.M.
4. I'll take you to the bank in the morning.
5. We have quizzes every Thursday.
6. The bank closes in ten minutes.

Exercise 113

3. the gym since this morning
4. for six weeks
5. can take care of your baby until
6. since she was born

7. until he loses ten pounds
8. in New York from 1996 to 2001
9. at the computer until lunch *or* . . . until I had lunch
10. in Philadelphia since she got married
11. married from 1997 to 2002

Exercise 114

3. After; finish my exercises
4. didn't speak (did not speak) to each other for 14
5. lock the doors before; go to bed
6. While they were neighbors
7. need to concentrate during
8. worked on the exam for three hours
9. always brush my teeth after
10. got sick while *or* got sick while she was
11. dream during

Exercise 115

2. in
3. in
4. at
5. on
6. in
7. on
8. on
9. at
10. at
11. at *or* in
12. in
13. on
14. in
15. at
16. in
17. at
18. in
19. in
20. at
21. at
22. at
23. in
24. on
25. in

Exercise 116

The sentences will vary.
Sample answers:

2. on; on *or* at
   I'd rather live (I would rather live) on the first floor of a building.
3. at; on *or* at
   I'd rather spend (I would rather spend) time at a concert.
4. in; in
   I'd rather be (I would rather be) in college.

5. at; at
   I'd rather exercise (I would rather exercise) at the gym.
6. in; on
   I'd rather sleep (I would rather sleep) in a bed.
7. in; in; in
   I'd rather live (I would rather live) in a big city.
8. on; in
   I'd rather take (I would rather take) a long trip in a car.
9. in *or* at; at
   I'd rather stay (I would rather stay) in a hotel.
10. in; on
    I'd rather eat (I would rather eat) on the balcony.
11. at *or* in; in *or* at
    I would rather spend free time in a museum.
12. in; in
    I'd rather swim (I would rather swim) in a pool.

Exercise 117

3. go to the bank
4. 's going (is going) home now
5. gets home
6. arrived at the mall
7. sitting in his car
8. is in the parking lot
9. 's going to return (is going to return) to the police station
10. go to school
11. got to the mall
12. came to the mall
13. is at school
14. gets home

Exercise 118

2. He is holding flowers under the table.
3. The couple's table is by the window. *or* . . . is next to the window.
4. The big table is in the middle.
5. There is a light above the table.
6. The children are sitting across from each other.
7. There are two small tables on the left.
8. There is a mouse under one of the tables.
9. The cook is standing in back of the waiter.
10. The busboy is in front of the cook and the waiter.
11. A woman is checking her makeup in front of the mirror. *or* . . . makeup in the mirror.
12. The mirror is next to the restrooms. *or* . . . by the restrooms.
13. The telephone is between the restrooms.

Exercise 119

3. Do you think I should hang this picture over the sofa?
4. Don't put your feet on the sofa. You'll make it dirty.
5. I walked out of the house, I felt a light rain.

6. Don't get out of the car here – there's too much traffic. Wait until I park the car.
7. We walked up the hill to the house at the top.
8. Water freezes when the temperature is under zero degrees Celsius.
9. We sat under a big tree and had a picnic.
10. You should turn on your car lights when you drive through a tunnel.
11. If you're warm, why don't you jump into the pool?
12. The thief ran out of the police station to escape.
13. My apartment is on the fifth floor. Be careful when you walk up the stairs.
14. The Smiths are going to Australia next week. They've never been there before.
15. I had to drive around the hospital four times before I found a parking place.
16. The door is locked. Let's go in the house through the window.
17. You can't get to San Francisco if you don't drive over this bridge.
18. We didn't notice the barber shop even though we walked past it three times.
19. Let's take our shoes off and walk along the beach.
20. Take the dishes out of the cabinet. It's time to set the table for dinner.

Exercise 120

2. it with this knife
3. young men with long hair
4. books by Mark Twain
5. leave home without your briefcase
6. any questions about the lesson
7. a foreign language on the phone
8. by a new teacher
9. with scissors
10. our homework with a pen
11. anything good on TV
12. by a famous artist
13. about the accident on the radio
14. At what age
15. by car or on foot
16. with sugar; without [sugar]
17. by bike; on time

Exercise 121

3. of big animals
4. at you
5. of people
6. to Gloria
7. of him
8. in going with us
9. of counting money all day
10. from his sister
11. at paying bills
12. at doing math problems
13. about the accident
14. at me

Exercise 122

3. is looking for
4. is thinking about/of going
5. depends on
6. written to *or* written
7. to call David
8. to take care of

Exercise 123

Answers will vary.
Sample answers:

1. I was in bed at 5 o'clock in the morning when a loud noise woke me.
2. My parents have been married for many years; they got married in 1970.
3. Not many people shop at the supermarket in my country on Friday mornings.
4. My brother often gets home at midnight on the weekend.
5. I haven't called my mother in two weeks.
6. The boss will be back on Monday.
7. I always brush my teeth before going to bed.
8. While I was waiting for a friend at school, I studied English grammar.
9. I'm working from 9 A.M. to 2 P.M. only, so I can meet you for a movie later this afternoon.
10. I like to eat popcorn while I watch a movie.
11. In some small towns in Italy, people aren't allowed to drive cars, so they travel around the town on bicycles.

Exercise 124

2. about
3. to
4. on
5. through
6. over
7. around
8. next to
9. under
10. past
11. on
12. in front of
13. with
14. at
15. at
16. X
17. in
18. without
19. out of
20. for
21. to
22. of
23. about *or* of
24. about
25. about
26. on
27. on
28. at
29. of

Exercise 125

2. looked out
3. come in
4. running away
5. gone away
6. went on
7. got into
8. drove off
9. grew up
10. gets along
11. kept on
12. come back
13. stood up
14. came back

Exercise 126

2. put them away
3. try them on
4. Look it up
5. take them back
6. threw it away
7. wake them up
8. tear them down
9. bring them back
10. gave it up *or* has given it up

Exercise 127

4. He went shopping because he needs new clothes. *or* . . . he needed new clothes.
5. He bought new pants and looked at shoes. *or* He bought new pants, and he looked at shoes.
6. didn't fit (did not fit), so he didn't get (did not get) any
7. He can wear a jacket to work, or he can wear a shirt and tie.
8. He started a new job last week, and his old clothes weren't (were not) very nice.
9. He likes the work, but he doesn't know (does not know) the other people very well.
10. He can work ten hours a day four days a week, or he can work eight hours a day five days a week.
11. He is new, so he doesn't (does not get) a vacation for six months.

Exercise 128

3. when we had the baby
4. while you were away
5. until he's (he is) better
6. when I get to Moscow
7. before you get a driver's license
8. while the radio is playing

9. When I'm (I am) tired
10. until I saw it

Exercise 129

A.

3. you stay in bed
4. We won't finish (will not finish) our work
5. I don't have to work (do not have to work)
6. he'll understand (he will understand)

B.

2. be sorry if you buy that car.
3. be more comfortable if you wear a jacket
4. 'll get (will get) a driver's license when she is 16

Exercise 130

3. it were nice
4. if I had
5. she would pass
6. if I could [play a musical instrument]
7. If she could [drive me to work]
8. we'd win (we would win) *or* we could win
9. I would take care of him
10. I wouldn't go (would not go) to the store again

Exercise 131

2. c
3. b
4. a
5. c
6. c
7. c
8. a
9. c

Exercise 132

Answers will vary.
Sample answers:
1. I can get a better job in sales
2. if I were in trouble with the police
3. you'll have to borrow money from someone
4. if I didn't finish college
5. call me late at night
6. my cousins in Norway; I have enough money
7. people would be happier
8. they didn't worry about money
9. their friend from Brazil comes for a visit
10. I'll call tonight.
11. I'd buy you a new DVD player
12. you will get into trouble
13. get to work a little late
14. if I didn't feel really sick
15. I always carry an umbrella with me

Exercise 133

3. which/that was on my desk
4. You should carry the boxes which/that are marked fragile
5. The bird which/that flew in the window was hard to catch.
6. I have an intelligent friend who can speak many languages.
7. A lawyer is a professional who helps people with legal problems.
8. The man who said he could speak thirteen languages was a liar.
9. The river which/that flows through London is called the Thames.
10. The countries which/that have borders with the United States are Canada and Mexico.

Exercise 134

3. a daughter he hasn't seen for a long time
4. His daughter married a doctor she met in a hospital in a village in India.
5. The village his daughter and her husband live in is in the high mountains.
6. They have two children the man has seen only a few times.
7. The children go to a school they love in New Delhi.
8. The man we talked to at the party is going to visit his daughter and her family soon.

Exercise 135

4. where you work *or* you work at
5. you bought this morning
6. that was destroyed last year
7. we were looking at
8. who lived next door to us in Tokyo
9. we waited two hours for
10. I am taking this semester
11. we stayed at on vacation

Exercise 136

Answers will vary.
Sample answers:
1. come and see you today, I'll come tomorrow for sure.
2. pay my bills, I'd borrow money from my parents
3. have a car, I have to ask friends to drive me places
4. I asked my neighbors not to play the loud music
5. many people go to the city beach
6. I'll go to the beach tomorrow
7. have a family reunion; we can get most of our relatives to come
8. refuse me help; I needed it

9. I have; writes me an e-mail every day;
10. My friend Sue is; like to be with
11. The accident was; driver couldn't avoid
12. A new carpet is; really need for our new apartment
13. Don't eat all the cake
14. New York is; people hurry all the time
15. New York; I spent my childhood
16. don't cost a lot of money
17. are very crowded
18. you have to wear formal clothes
19. I didn't have time to give it to her
20. The child saw the monkeys

Exercise 137

3. she thought only about the past, she wouldn't be (would not be) so happy
4. she saves enough money, she'll go (will go) to China
5. She doesn't work (does not work) in the garden; it rains
6. She'll be (She will be) in her garden at 7 A.M. tomorrow; it's not raining / it isn't raining (it is not raining)
7. she weren't (were not) so busy and active, she wouldn't (would not) be happy.
8. she lost hope, she wouldn't be (would not be) happy
9. She probably wouldn't have as many friends; she weren't (were not) so sociable